KAUAI TRAVEL GUIDE

(The Garden Isle)

Discovering the Beauty, Top-Attractions, Best Time to Visit, Expert Tips, and Essential Know-How for an Unforgettable Vacation

Special
30 BEST PLACE TO
VISIT AND WHEN

James D. Vollmer

TABLE OF CONTENTS

KAUAI EXPERIENCE

Arriving on the shores of Kauai felt like stepping into a dream I never wanted to wake up from. The warm breeze greeted me like an old friend, carrying the scent of the ocean and the promise of adventure. As I explored the island's diverse landscapes, from the rugged cliffs of the Na Pali Coast to the serene beaches that seemed to stretch on forever, I knew I was in for an unforgettable journey.

Engaging with the locals revealed a deep sense of aloha that radiated from every interaction. From the moment I attempted my first "Mahalo" to the gracious smiles that followed, I felt like a part of their close-knit community. Learning about the island's history, traditions, and significance ignited a spark within me. It was more than just a vacation; it was a connection to a culture that embraced me as one of its own.

My days were a mix of exploration and relaxation, each revealing a new facet of Kauai's charm. I hiked through dense rainforests to discover hidden waterfalls that seemed straight out of a fairy tale. I watched the sun dip below the horizon at the enchanting Hanalei Bay, painting the sky with hues I never knew existed. Snorkeling in crystal-clear waters brought me face-to-face with vibrant marine life, reminding me of the intricate balance of nature.

It was during a helicopter tour over the island that I truly understood its magnificence. From above, I witnessed the intricate patterns of the Napali Coast, the untouched beauty of Waimea Canyon, and the emerald valleys that stretched as far as the eye could see. The pilot's narration painted a vivid picture of Kauai's history, its unique microclimates, and its contributions to the film industry. It was a moment of awe that stirred something within me.

As my vacation drew to a close, I found myself jotting down notes, capturing moments, and envisioning a guide that could help others experience the magic of Kauai. I wanted to share the feeling of standing atop the Sleeping Giant Trail at sunrise, the taste of fresh fruits from the local farmers' market, and the joy of connecting with fellow travelers over the island's rich culture. The idea for the "Kauai Travel Guide" began to take shape.

Leaving Kauai was bittersweet, but I knew it wasn't a goodbye. The island had woven its spell around me, and I promised myself that I would return. As I boarded the plane, I felt a sense of purpose and excitement. I was determined to create a guide that would capture the essence of Kauai, offer valuable insights, and inspire others to embark on their own journey of discovery.

So here it is, the "Kauai Travel Guide," born out of a traveler's passion for sharing the beauty, the stories, and the soul of this remarkable island. My experience on Kauai has left an indelible mark on my heart, and I can't wait to return, armed with the insights and knowledge to dive even deeper into the enchanting world of the Garden Isle. Until then, my fellow adventurers, may your journey be as magical as mine was. Aloha!

Night street view

Introduction

Kauai, The Garden Isle

Welcome to Kauai, the Garden Isle, a paradise tucked in the middle of the Hawaiian archipelago. This travel book is meant to be your ultimate companion, giving you a complete overview of all you need to know about Kauai before, during, and after your stay. Whether you are a seasoned tourist or going on your first Hawaiian journey, Kauai provides an unrivaled combination of natural beauty, cultural richness, and adventurous spirit that will capture your senses and leave you with treasured memories.

Discovering Kauai

Kauai is an island of wonder, famed for its lush scenery, clean beaches, and dramatic coastlines. The oldest of the Hawaiian Islands, Kauai, is a geological masterpiece shaped by millennia of volcanic activity and weathering.

As you tour the island, you will find gushing waterfalls, green valleys, and lush rainforests that have given it the moniker "The Garden Isle."

Beyond its magnificent natural beauty, Kauai possesses a distinct cultural legacy strongly entrenched in the traditions of the native Hawaiian people. The island's welcome aloha atmosphere, exhibited via hula performances, colorful festivals, and warm hospitality, will engulf you in a feeling of belonging. Additionally, Kauai provides a wealth of interesting activities, like snorkeling in pristine seas, trekking to hidden views, and tasting the island's wonderful food.

What to Expect From This Travel Guide

This expertly designed travel book includes all the critical information you need to make the most of your vacation to Kauai, the Garden Isle. Divided into well-structured chapters, the book covers every facet of your adventure. It opens with an introduction, offering a brief summary of Kauai's history, geography, culture, and why it's a perfect vacation. Understanding national laws and local traditions is essential for a courteous stay.

Practical guidance on reaching and traversing the island is offered in the "Getting to and Around Kauai" section. Visa procedures, housing alternatives, and discovering Kauai's distinctive food are covered.

Uncover popular attractions, manage your wallet, and remain safe with complete safety recommendations. Learn about the best time to travel, health precautions, and emergency assistance.

Discover the island's charm and attractions, navigate with travel advice and etiquette, and support sustainable tourism. The book also gives typical words and expressions in the local language to enrich your cultural experience.

With this book in hand, you're all ready for an amazing adventure in Kauai.

Making the Best Use of This Travel Guide

Before Your Trip

- Read through the full guide to educate yourself on Kauai's history, culture, and attractions.
- Research certain areas of interest in depth and organize your trip appropriately.
- Check visa requirements and other entrance information for overseas visitors.
- Make lodging bookings well in advance.

During Your Vacation

- Carry a paper or digital copy of the handbook for convenient reference.
- Use the following safety guidelines and health information to ensure safe and pleasurable travel.
- Keep track of the locations you visit and your experiences using the guide's suggestions.

After Your Trip

- Reflect on your trip and share your experiences with family and friends.
- Provide comments on the guide's efficacy to help improve future versions.
- Cherish the memories and contemplate a return trip to Kauai in the future.

With this travel guide in hand, you are ready to go on a memorable experience in Kauai.

Embrace the aloha spirit, immerse yourself in the island's splendor, and let the breathtaking scenery and lively culture of Kauai leave an unforgettable impact on your soul. Mahalo and have a nice voyage!

Chapter One

About Kauai: The Garden Isle

Kauai, popularly referred to as "The Garden Isle," is an enchanted paradise situated in the Pacific Ocean and is the oldest of the Hawaiian Islands. Known for its lush green landscapes, breathtaking waterfalls, clean beaches, and varied flora and fauna, Kauai is a refuge for nature lovers and adventure seekers alike. This gorgeous island covers over 550 square miles and is the fourth-largest among the Hawaiian Islands.

Kauai's natural beauty is unparalleled, with dramatic cliffs along the Napali Coast, the serene Wailua River, and the iconic Waimea Canyon, often called the "Grand Canyon of the Pacific." The island's untouched wilderness and vibrant ecosystems make it a remarkable destination for ecotourism and sustainable travel.

A Brief History of Kauai

The history of Kauai is entrenched in rich cultural traditions and tales. The earliest inhabitants to come to the island were

Polynesian voyagers who traveled from other Pacific islands between the years 300 and 600 A.D. These early immigrants brought their habits, language, and agricultural techniques with them, laying the groundwork for Kauai's distinct culture.

The history of the island includes the reign of King Kaumuali'i, Kauai's last independent king, who faced enormous challenges when the island was seized by King Kamehameha I of Hawaii in 1810. Despite its annexation, Kauai has retained much of its original character and continues to celebrate its original traditions and customs.

Language Spoken in Kauai

English is the official language of Kauai and the greater state of Hawaii. However, the Hawaiian language, known as 'Olelo Hawai'i,' has major cultural value and is widely spoken and taught in schools to preserve the local heritage. Visitors to Kauai commonly encounter Hawaiian terms in place names, street signs, and customary greetings, developing a stronger connection to the island's cultural heritage.

Currency and Money matter

As a part of the United States, the official currency of Kauai is the US Dollar (USD). ATMs are frequently accessible in major cities and tourist locations, making it easier for visitors to acquire cash. Credit cards are commonly accepted at most businesses, although it is wise to carry sufficient cash for smaller vendors or in an emergency.

Geographical Details of Kauai

Kauai's geographical characteristics are nothing short of magnificent. The island is marked by its harsh landscape, with the towering cliffs of the Napali Coast on the northwest side and the beautiful Waimea Canyon on the western end. The middle half of the island is characterized by lush valleys and mountains, while the east coast features spectacular waterfalls and rich plains.

Mount Waialeale, situated near the middle of the island, is one of the wettest spots on Earth, contributing to the profusion of rainforests and green vistas that have given Kauai its moniker, "The Garden Isle."

Ethnicity and Socio-cultural

Kauai's diversified population encompasses a combination of cultures, including Native Hawaiians, Asians, Caucasians, and Pacific Islanders. The island's eclectic background is reflected in its art, food, music, and festivals.

The spirit of 'Aloha,' which incorporates love, compassion, and oneness, is a vital part of Kauai's socio-cultural life. The villagers greet guests with warmth and generosity, asking them to engage in traditional rites and festivals.

Reasons to Travel to Kauai

1. Breathtaking Natural Beauty: Kauai's scenery is a photographer's dream come true. From the craggy shoreline of the Napali Coast to the spectacular panoramas of Waimea Canyon, each part of the island provides a beautiful treasure to discover.

2. Outdoor Adventures: For outdoor aficionados, Kauai is a wonderland. Hiking, kayaking, snorkeling, surfing, and zip-lining are just a few of the adventurous activities accessible to immerse oneself in nature's beauties.

3. Cultural Immersion: Discover the rich history and cultural legacy of Kauai via its ancient temples, museums, traditional hula performances, and storytelling sessions.

4. Relaxation and Tranquility: Kauai's laid-back environment and peaceful beaches provide the ideal backdrop for relaxation and renewal.

5. Delicious Cuisine: Indulge in a gastronomic voyage of local delicacies, from fresh seafood to classic Hawaiian specialties like poi and kalua pig.

6. Opulent Resorts and Accommodations: Kauai provides a broad selection of lodging alternatives, including opulent resorts, attractive boutique hotels, and lovely vacation rentals.

7. Napali Coast Exploration: Embark on a boat excursion or stroll along the Napali Coast to observe its stunning cliffs and secret sea caves.

8. A Lovely Getaway: With its lovely sunsets and quiet locations, Kauai is a favorite destination for couples seeking a romantic retreat.

In the following chapters, we will dig further into Kauai's offerings, including its intriguing attractions, travel suggestions, safety requirements, and much more, to ensure you have a memorable and enlightening trip on The Garden Isle.

Chapter Two

Country Laws and Local Customs

Understanding Local Laws and Regulations

Kauai, being part of the state of Hawaii, follows the legal framework of the United States, but it also has particular local rules and regulations that tourists need to be aware of throughout their stay. Understanding and observing these regulations is vital to having a safe and pleasurable trip on the island.

Legal System and Jurisdiction

The legal system of Kauai is modeled on the U.S. Constitution and functions under a common law framework. Local law enforcement authorities and courts enforce the state's laws and regulations. The County of Kauai has a police department responsible for ensuring public safety and upholding the law. In the event of any legal concerns during your visit, you will be subject to the jurisdiction of the state and municipal courts.

Alcohol and Tobacco Laws

The legal drinking age in Kauai, like in the rest of the United States, is 21. It is vital to possess a proper ID, such as a driver's license or passport, to show your age while buying alcoholic drinks. Drinking in public areas, except at licensed businesses, is typically illegal. Additionally, smoking rules are tight in Hawaii, and smoking is not permitted in most indoor public locations, including hotels, restaurants, and bars.

Drug Laws

Kauai has strong drug regulations that coincide with federal laws in the United States. Possession, distribution, or use of illicit narcotics is a serious violation and may lead to severe consequences, including imprisonment. It is vital to avoid any interaction with illicit narcotics throughout your time on Kauai.

Traffic Laws

Driving in Kauai is comparable to driving in the rest of the U.S., with traffic driving on the right-hand side of the road. Speed limits and other traffic restrictions are closely enforced, and traffic offenses may result in penalties and points on your driver's license. It is crucial to respect traffic regulations and be aware of pedestrian crosswalks since pedestrian safety is a priority.

Environmental Laws

Kauai is home to varied and sensitive ecosystems, and the island has strong environmental protection regulations to conserve its natural beauty. Visitors are urged to practice Leave No Trace principles by avoiding littering and protecting wildlife and marine life. Certain regions may have limited access or need permissions for specified activities to underestimate human effects on the environment.

Respecting Kauai's Culture and Traditions

Kauai, like the rest of Hawaii, has a rich cultural past strongly steeped in the customs and traditions of its original Hawaiian people. As a guest, it is crucial to respect and honor the local culture to recognize the island's actual spirit and build a healthy connection with its inhabitants.

Kapu (Taboos) and Sacred Sites

Many locations on Kauai possess important cultural and spiritual values for the Hawaiian people. Some locales may be recognized as holy sites, and it is vital to know and abide by any kapu (taboos) linked with such places. Signs may indicate limited access, and visitors are urged to comply with these limitations to maintain the cultural integrity of these places.

Aloha Spirit

The notion of "Aloha" is important to Hawaiian culture. Aloha implies love, compassion, and a real connection with people.

When dealing with natives, adopting the Aloha attitude and displaying respect and friendliness will be immensely welcomed.

Language and Cultural Etiquette

While English is commonly used on the island, learning a few Hawaiian terms and phrases may demonstrate your appreciation for the local culture. Addressing someone with courtesy titles, such as "Aunty" or "Uncle" for the elderly, is a customary expression of respect in Hawaiian society.

Cultural Events and Practices

Participating in cultural events and activities may be a gratifying experience. Attending a traditional Hawaiian ceremony or luau might give insight into the island's history and culture.

However, it is crucial to observe and follow any instructions presented during these activities to be culturally aware.

Preservation of Natural Resources

Kauai's cultural customs are directly related to the environment. Visitors are advised to be careful of their influence on the island's natural resources.

For example, abstaining from touching or collecting antiques or natural specimens and avoiding harming marine life during snorkeling or diving expeditions

Understanding Kauai's national laws and respecting its local traditions are key components of being a responsible and conscientious guest. By familiarizing yourself with the legislative structure and cultural traditions of the island, you can assure a pleasant and enjoyable experience throughout your visit.

Embracing the spirit of Aloha and demonstrating respect for the natural and cultural history of Kauai will not only improve your experience but also contribute to the preservation of this gorgeous island for future generations of visitors to enjoy.

Chapter Three

Getting to and Around Kauai

Kauai, the Garden Isle, is a charming Hawaiian paradise famed for its breathtaking scenery, clean beaches, and rich cultural history. Navigating this gorgeous island swiftly and cost-effectively is crucial for a pleasant visit. In this comprehensive chapter, we will delve into the best ways to reach Kauai, explore various transportation options on the island, provide valuable tips for getting around safely and economically, and outline the costs associated with each mode of transportation to help you plan your Kauai adventure wisely.

1. Best Ways to Reach Kauai

Flights to Kauai

Traveling by flight is the most popular method to reach Kauai. The Lihue Airport (LIH) is the principal entrance to the island, receiving direct flights from major international airports in the United States, including Los Angeles, San Francisco, Seattle, and Honolulu. The cost of a flight might vary based on your departure location and the time of year.

Booking your flights in advance and being flexible with trip dates will help you get more reasonable rates.

Inter-island Flights

If you're already in Hawaii and desire to visit Kauai from another island, inter-island flights are a simple choice. Flights from Honolulu (Oahu) to Lihue (Kauai) are frequent and often fairly priced, particularly when booked long in advance.

Cruise Ships

Some tourists choose cruise ships that include Kauai as a port of call. While the cost of a cruise may vary widely depending on the cruise line, cabin type, and length, these packages frequently give an all-inclusive experience with meals, lodgings, and onboard activities included.

Private Yachts and Charters

For those wanting a premium and intimate experience, arriving on Kauai by private boat or charter is an option. The expense of private charters might be high, but they provide a unique and personal opportunity to tour the island at your own speed.

2. Transportation Options on the Island

Rental Cars

Renting a vehicle is strongly advised for touring Kauai at your own speed. The island's road network is well-maintained, and owning a vehicle offers you the opportunity to explore off-the-beaten-path spots. Rental car rates vary depending on the vehicle type, rental period, and demand. On average, daily fees might vary from $40 to $150 or more.

Public Transportation

The Kauai Bus is an economical alternative for travelling across the island. A one-way ride normally costs about $2, while day passes are available for roughly $10. The bus links major cities and attractions, making it an inexpensive alternative for budget-conscious vacationers.

Taxis and Rideshare Services

Taxis are accessible on the island, mostly stationed near the airport and major resort districts. Rideshare services like Uber and Lyft also operate on Kauai, enabling convenient and frequently cost-effective transportation within popular areas.

Bicycles and Scooter

Exploring Kauai on two wheels is an eco-friendly and exciting choice. Bike rentals start at roughly $20 per day, while scooter rentals may vary from $30 to $60 per day, depending on the model of scooter and rental period.

3. Getting Around Safely and Economically

Island Road Network

Kauai's road network spans most of the island, giving access to significant attractions. The Kaumualii Highway (Route 50) and the Kuhio Highway (Route 56) are the primary roadways linking diverse locations. Plan your journey in a manner that avoids backtracking to maximize time and save fuel expenses.

Self-Driving

If you choose to rent an automobile, familiarize yourself with local driving restrictions and road signs. Drive with care, particularly on narrow and twisting roads, and be cautious of pedestrians and animals.

Parking

spaces are accessible at most motels and tourist attractions. Some attractions may charge a modest parking fee, generally ranging from $5 to $10.

Shared Transportation

Carpooling with other visitors or joining group excursions not only cuts expenses but also lessens the environmental impact of transportation.

Local Transportation on Kauai

When visiting the lovely island of Kauai, effective local transportation is vital for making the most of your stay. I present a thorough guide to travelling around the island, including public transit alternatives, auto rentals, and driving advice.

Getting Around the Island

Kauai is a very tiny island, with an area of around 552 square miles, making it easier to traverse and explore. There are numerous transportation choices available, enabling you to see the island's different landscapes and attractions.

Public Transportation Options

Kauai Bus

The Kauai Bus is the principal public transportation service on the island, run by the County of Kauai. It provides an economical and eco-friendly method to travel between major attractions, including towns, beaches, retail centers, and other significant areas of interest. The buses are air-conditioned and fitted with bike racks, making them comfortable for bikers.

It's vital to acquaint yourself with the Kauai Bus timetable and routes before utilizing the service. Buses may not be as regular as in bigger cities, so planning your route in advance might help you make the most of your time.

Shared Ride Services

On Kauai, you may also discover shared transportation services comparable to ride-hailing applications present in other places. These services provide door-to-door transportation, allowing additional flexibility in terms of pickup and drop-off locations. Using these services might be a useful choice for those who want a more customized and timely way of traveling around the island.

Car Rentals and Driving Tips

Car Rentals

Renting a vehicle is one of the most popular transportation alternatives on Kauai since it enables you to explore the island at your own leisure and visit more hidden areas that may not be accessible by public transit. Car rental firms may be located at the Lihue Airport and in the main cities, providing a selection of cars to meet your requirements.

When renting a rental vehicle, consider reserving in advance, particularly during busy tourist seasons, to obtain the best pricing and assure availability. Also, make sure to examine the rental company's policy on insurance coverage and other costs.

Driving Tips

Driving on Kauai gives a terrific chance to take in the island's magnificent beauty, but it's vital to keep some driving recommendations in mind:

-Observe Speed restrictions: Respect the established speed restrictions, which may vary on various roadways. Be extra careful on twisting coastal roads and through residential neighborhoods.

- Use Pullouts: Kauai's breathtaking splendor can encourage you to stop often for photographs. When doing so, utilize designated pullouts to prevent impeding traffic.

- Beware of Weather Conditions: The weather on Kauai may change swiftly, particularly in regions with higher altitudes. Be prepared for rain, fog, or other weather conditions and alter your driving accordingly.

- One-Lane Bridges: Some rural regions include one-lane bridges. Yield to approaching vehicles and respect any posted signs stating right-of-way restrictions.

- Respect fauna: Kauai's fauna, including hens and roosters, are known to wander freely. Be careful and avoid abrupt stops or swerves to avert accidents.

- Parking: When parking, ensure you adhere to all parking restrictions to prevent penalties or towing.

- Gas Stations: Gas stations are mostly situated in towns and around the airport. If traveling on a longer trip, ensure you have enough gasoline to reach your goal and return.

- Navigation: Cell phone coverage may be restricted in certain isolated places. Consider utilizing offline maps or getting a real map to aid with navigation.

- Emergency Assistance: In case of an emergency, call 911 for quick aid.

Getting to know Kauai is a key component of any vacation to the Garden Isle.

Top-Rated Car Rental Companies

To aid you in making the best decision for your travel requirements, I have produced a list of the top-rated transport firms in Kauai. These companies have been highly recommended by visitors for their dependable service, high client satisfaction, and dedication to providing a pleasant and memorable experience.

Whether you prefer guided excursions, rental automobiles, or shared transportation, these reliable providers have got you covered:

a. Enterprise Rent-A-vehicle: Enterprise is a well-known vehicle rental firm with many facilities around Kauai, including the Lihue Airport. They provide a broad fleet of vehicles, from budget cars to SUVs, guaranteeing that you will discover the appropriate vehicle for your island excursions.

b. Budget Car Rental: Budget Car Rental is a popular option among travelers seeking reasonable pricing and reliable service. They provide convenient pick-up and drop-off sites, making it simple to begin your adventure straight after arriving.

c. Avis Car Rental: Avis is another trustworthy car rental provider that offers a broad range of automobiles, including convertible variants, to enhance your gorgeous drives along Kauai's shores.

Top-Rated Guided Tour Companies

a. Blue Hawaiian Helicopters

Offering exhilarating helicopter flights, Blue Hawaiian Helicopters enables you to view Kauai's outstanding natural sights from a unique airborne perspective. Their expert pilots deliver educational and amusing comments during the journey.

b. Kauai ATV: For those seeking adrenaline-fueled experiences, Kauai ATV provides amazing off-road ATV rides across the island's harsh terrain, leading you to secret waterfalls and magnificent landscapes.

c. Kauai Sea Trips: Specializing in catamaran excursions and boat trips along the Napali Coast, Kauai Sea Tours gives an unparalleled experience of the island's magnificent sea cliffs, sea caves, and aquatic life.

Top-Rated Public Transportation

a. The Kauai Bus: The official public transportation system on the island, The Kauai Bus provides economical and convenient services, linking major towns and notable sites. It's a good choice for budget-conscious vacationers.

Top-Rated Rideshare Services

a. Uber: Uber operates on Kauai, providing quick and efficient transportation throughout major towns and tourism regions. The app-based service enables you to request trips with simplicity.

b. Lyft: Lyft is another ridesharing service present on the island, providing an alternative to regular taxis and public transit.

Top-Rated Bicycle and Scooter Rentals

a. Kauai Cycle: Kauai Cycle provides bicycle rentals for exploring the island's gorgeous pathways and trails. They offer excellent bikes and safety gear to provide a fun and safe riding experience.

b. Kauai Mopeds and Scooters: For those who prefer two-wheeled adventures, Kauai Mopeds and Scooters provides scooter rentals, providing a fun and eco-friendly way to navigate around Kauai.

Remember to reserve your transportation in advance, particularly during busy tourist seasons, to guarantee your chosen method of transit and ensure a flawless voyage on the Garden Isle.

Exploring Kauai needs careful preparation to create a smooth and pleasurable trip. While the cost of transportation might vary, picking the most acceptable method of transportation depending on your budget and preferences is vital.

Whether you want to hire a vehicle for the convenience and flexibility it provides or choose public transit to economize on expenditures, Kauai's breathtaking beauty and lively culture are guaranteed to capture your heart. Always emphasize safety and be careful of the environment when traveling to this gorgeous Garden Isle. Aloha and safe travels!

Chapter Four

Visa Requirements and Entry Information

Journeying to the Garden Isle is a dream come true for many explorers and vacation seekers. However, before beginning this voyage, it's vital to grasp the visa requirements and entrance processes, depending on your nation of origin. This chapter will offer you in-depth knowledge and comprehension of the visa requirements for travelers from the UK, Asia, Europe, and other continents, as well as essential information on the entrance procedure and official resources for visa applications and queries

Visa Requirements for Travelers from the UK

If you are a citizen of the United Kingdom and want to visit Kauai, you may be asking about the visa requirements for your trip. Fortunately, wanderers from the UK are given visa-free access to the United States for short-term trips, including travel to Kauai. The Visa Waiver Program (VWP) permits UK nationals to remain in the US, including Hawaii, for up to 90 days without having a visa.

To take advantage of the VWP, you must apply for the Electronic System for Travel Authorization (ESTA) before your travel. The ESTA is an automated mechanism used to evaluate the eligibility of visitors under the VWP and must be completed online. It is crucial to apply for the ESTA well in advance of your trip dates, since approvals may take up to 72 hours. Once accepted, your ESTA is normally good for several trips over a two-year period or until your passport expires.

It's vital to realize that the ESTA is not a visa, but rather a license to travel visa-free under the VWP. It is necessary to carry a printed copy of your authorized ESTA throughout your visit to the United States, since you may be requested to provide it upon arrival.

Visa Requirements for Travelers from Asia

For tourists from many countries in Asia, including China, Japan, India, and others, the visa requirements for visiting Kauai may vary based on your nationality. The United States has distinct visa restrictions for different Asian nations, and it's vital to visit the US Department of State website or speak with the US embassy or consulate in your home country for the most up-to-date information.

In general, many Asian nations are not part of the Visa Waiver Program, which means tourists will need to apply for a B-1 (Business) or B-2 (Tourism) visiting visa. These visas are often provided for short-term visits, enabling tourists to visit Kauai for tourism, business meetings, or other acceptable objectives.

The visa application procedure may be long; therefore, it is advised to apply well in advance of your scheduled trip dates. You will need to make an appointment at the US embassy or consulate and provide different papers, including a valid passport, evidence of links to your home country, a trip itinerary, financial documents, and a completed visa application form.

Keep in mind that visa criteria and application procedures may vary, so it's vital to remain informed of the newest information and requirements from official US government sources.

Visa Requirements for Travelers from Europe and Other Continents

Travelers from Europe and other continents, save those protected under the Visa Waiver Program, will normally need to get a B-1 or B-2 visa to visit Kauai.

Europe encompasses several nations, each with its own special visa restrictions, therefore, it is vital to visit the US Department of State website or speak with the US embassy or consulate in your own country for detailed information on visa requirements.

The visa application procedure normally entails making an appointment at the US embassy or consulate, completing the relevant paperwork, and presenting supporting documents, such as a valid passport, evidence of adequate cash for your trip, a travel schedule, and links to your home country.

Similar to tourists from Asia, it is essential to start the visa application procedure well in advance to prevent any last-minute issues that might compromise your trip plans.

Entry Information and Immigration Process

Upon arrival in Kauai, you will go through the US immigration and customs procedures since Hawaii is part of the United States.

The entry procedure entails submitting your passport and visa (if applicable) to US Customs and Border Protection personnel. They will question you about the purpose of your visit, and the length of your stay, and they may query about your lodgings and travel arrangements.

Be prepared to answer these questions accurately and clearly, as this will help guarantee a smooth admission into the nation. If you are traveling under the Visa Waiver Program, ensure you have a printed copy of your approved ESTA with you.

It is critical to be aware of all items prohibited by US customs, as failing to disclose restricted items may result in fines or other penalties. Agricultural goods, some drugs, and guns are examples of things that may be subject to limitations.

Official Resources for Visa Applications and Inquiries

To apply for visas or acquire correct and up-to-date information on entrance requirements and visa procedures, it is important to turn to official sources provided by the US government.

The US Department of State website (https://travel.state.gov) gives extensive and accurate information on visa categories, application methods, costs, and processing periods. This website is an excellent resource for visitors from across the globe.

For special concerns and help, travelers may also contact the US embassy or consulate in their home country.

These diplomatic posts are ready to address inquiries relating to visa applications and give information on the admission procedure.

Knowing the visa requirements and admission processes is an essential step in organizing a successful vacation to Kauai. Visitors from diverse nations, including the UK, Asia, Europe, and beyond, must be aware of their individual visa responsibilities and the necessity of conforming to US immigration regulations.

By obtaining the necessary visas and following official procedures, you can ensure a smooth and enjoyable visit while exploring the breathtaking beauty of Kauai, the Garden Isle.

Chapter Five

Accommodation Options

When planning a vacation to the lovely island of Kauai, one of the most crucial items to consider is your hotel. Kauai provides a vast assortment of alternatives to fit any traveler's interests and tastes. From opulent resorts to budget-friendly alternatives, there is something for everyone on the Garden Isle.

Types of Accommodations Available

Kauai provides a varied choice of lodgings that appeal to different vacation tastes and budgets

1. Luxury Resorts

For travelers seeking the ultimate in extravagance and leisure, Kauai's luxury resorts are a wonderful option. These five-star resorts provide magnificent seaside sites, top-notch facilities, world-class spas, exquisite restaurants, and flawless service. Some of the most recognized luxury resorts on the island are the St. Regis Princeville Resort, the Grand Hyatt Kauai Resort and Spa, and the Four Seasons Resort at Ko Olina.

2. Hotels and Inns

Kauai is home to a collection of hotels and inns that vary from mid-range to upmarket. These lodgings often feature nice rooms, on-site food choices, and facilities to guarantee a pleasurable stay. Popular alternatives include the Kauai Marriott Resort in Lihue, the Sheraton Kauai Resort in Poipu, and the Waimea Plantation Cottages on the west side of the island.

3. Vacation Rentals

Embrace the real spirit of aloha by staying in a vacation rental, which might be an apartment, condominium, cottage, or villa. Vacation rentals provide the comfort of a home away from home, with fully equipped kitchens, private facilities, and the flexibility to accommodate larger parties or families. Websites like Airbnb and VRBO provide a broad choice of holiday homes around the island.

4. Bed and Breakfasts

For a more private and customized experience, try a stay at a beautiful bed and breakfast. These quaint lodgings are typically hosted by local individuals who may give significant insights into the island's culture and hidden jewels. The Hanalei Bay Bed

& Breakfast in Hanalei and the Kauai Country Inn in Lihue are popular alternatives for guests wanting a B&B experience.

5. Hostels and Guesthouses

Budget-conscious guests will discover a few hostels and guesthouses dispersed around the island. These alternatives provide shared lodgings and community areas, making them great for single travelers or those wishing to interact with other adventurers.

Top Areas to Stay on the Island

The island of Kauai is separated into numerous sections, each with its own particular beauty and attractions. When picking your lodging, consider the following key areas

1. Poipu

Located on the sunny south coast, Poipu is a popular destination for its stunning beaches, good snorkeling locations, and a broad selection of housing options. It's a fantastic alternative for families and couples alike.

2. Princeville and Hanalei

On the verdant north coast, these locations provide stunning views of the ocean and mountains. Here, you'll discover luxurious resorts, vacation cottages, and a laid-back atmosphere great for relaxation.

3. Lihue

As the island's major town, Lihue provides a central position with easy access to many attractions. It's a handy location for seeing Kauai's different scenery and enjoying its facilities.

4. Kapaa

Situated on the east coast, Kapaa is recognized for its attractive small-town ambiance, quirky shops, and eateries. It's a terrific site for budget-friendly lodgings with access to both the north and south coastlines.

5. Hanapepe and Waimea

These settlements on the west side of the island give a look into Kauai's history and culture. Visitors may discover unusual housing alternatives and visit the adjacent Waimea Canyon, popularly known as the "Grand Canyon of the Pacific."

Budget-Friendly Accommodations

Travelers on a budget need not worry; Kauai provides many alternatives that won't break the bank:

1. Hostels: Kauai features a few hostels that offer dormitory-style rooms at moderate prices. The Kauai Beach House Hostel in Kapaa and the Kauai International Hostel in Lihue are popular alternatives for backpackers and budget travelers.

2. Budget Hotels & Inns: Several hotels and inns provide budget-friendly accommodations without sacrificing comfort. The Aston Islander on the Beach in Kapaa and the Tip Top Motel in Lihue are outstanding examples of competitively priced lodgings.

3. Vacation Rentals & Cottages: Opting for a vacation rental or cottage may be cost-effective, particularly for bigger parties or prolonged visits. Look for offers on websites like Airbnb, where you may locate nice apartments at inexpensive costs.

Choosing the Right Accommodation for Your Budget and Preferences

Selecting the best lodging for your Kauai journey needs careful consideration of your budget, travel style, and preferred activities. Here are some crucial recommendations to help you make the proper choice:

1. Define Your Budget: Before researching lodgings, determine a clear budget for your stay on the island. Consider how much you are willing to spend on lodging compared to your entire trip expenditures.

2. Identify Your Priorities: Determine the important things that matter most to you in your accommodation, such as closeness to the beach, on-site facilities, or a certain view.

3. Consider Location: Think about the locations you'd want to visit the most and select an accommodation that gives easy access to those attractions.

4. Read Reviews: Check out internet reviews from former guests to get a feel for the property's quality, cleanliness, and customer service.

5. Book in Advance: Secure your accommodations far ahead of your vacation dates, particularly during busy tourist seasons, to assure availability and maybe discover cheaper offers.

6. Contact the Property Directly: If you have particular inquiries or requests, don't hesitate to contact the accommodation directly for additional information.

Top 20 Highly-Rated Hotels in Kauai

1. Grand Hyatt Kauai Resort & Spa

A premium resort in Poipu, Grand Hyatt Kauai provides magnificent suites, lovely gardens, various pools, and access to Poipu Bay Golf Course. Address: 1571 Poipu Road, Poipu. Average cost: $400 - $800 per night.

2. Koa Kea Hotel & Resort

This boutique beachfront hotel in Poipu provides contemporary rooms, a tranquil pool area, and a soothing spa. Address: 2251 Poipu Road, Poipu. Average cost: $300 - $600 per night.

3. The Westin Princeville Ocean Resort Villas

Nestled in Princeville, this resort features large villas with spectacular views, access to neighboring beaches, and recreational amenities. Address: 3838 Wyllie Rd., Princeville Average cost: $250 - $500 per night.

4. Hanalei Colony Resort

Situated in Hanalei, this beachside resort provides tranquil and isolated rooms, ideal for visitors seeking a serene retreat. Address: 5-7130 Kuhio Hwy., Hanalei. Average cost: $300 - $600 per night.

5. Kauai Beach Resort

Located in Lihue, Kauai Beach Resort features a stunning beachside location and a variety of facilities. Guests may enjoy numerous swimming pools, waterslides, a spa, and different eating choices. Address: 4331 Kauai Beach Dr., Lihue. Average cost: $200 - $400 per night.

6. Sheraton Kauai Resort

Situated in Poipu, the Sheraton Kauai Resort provides luxurious accommodations with private lanais, ocean views, and access to Poipu Beach. Address: 2440 Hoonani Rd., Poipu. Average cost: $250 - $500 per night.

7. Kauai Marriott Resort

Located in Lihue, this resort boasts spacious accommodations, a championship golf course, a big pool area with a lazy river, and a peaceful spa. Address: 3610 Rice St., Lihue. Average cost: $300 - $600 per night.

8. The Cliffs in Princeville

These condo-style lodgings in Princeville give visitors .complete kitchens and access to different facilities, including tennis courts and swimming pools. Address: 3811 Edward   , Princeville. Average cost: $150 - $300 per night.

9. Aston Islander on the Beach

This beachfront hotel in Kapaa provides comfortable rooms with tropical designs, ocean views, and a pool area with a BBQ area. Address: 440 Aleka Pl., Kapaa. Average cost: $150 - $300 per night.

10. Koloa Landing Resort, near Poipu

A magnificent resort in Poipu, Koloa Landing provides big villas with contemporary facilities, various pools, and a superb spa. Address: 2641 Poipu Rd, Poipu. Average cost: $350 - $700 per night.

11. St. Regis Princeville Resort

Address: 5520 Ka Haku Rd, Princeville, HI 96722

Cost: Starting from $500 per night

12. Grand Hyatt Kauai Resort and Spa

Address: 1571 Poipu Rd, Koloa, HI 96756

Cost: Starting from $450 per night

13. Four Seasons Resort in Ko Olina

Address: 92-1001 Olani St, Kapolei, HI 96707

Cost: Starting from $600 per night

14. Kauai Marriott Resorts

Address: 3610 Rice St, Lihue, HI 96766

Cost: Starting from $300 per nigh

15. Sheraton Kauai Resort

Address: 2440 Hoonani Rd, Koloa, HI 96756

Cost: Starting at $350 per night

16. Waimea Plantation Cottages

Address: 9400 Kaumualii Hwy, Waimea, HI 96796

Cost: Starting from $250 per night

17. Hanalei Bay Bed & Breakfast

Address: 5380 Akalei Pl, Princeville, HI 96722

Cost: Starting from $200 per night

18. Kauai Country Inn

Address: 6440 Olohena Rd, Kapa'a, HI 96746

Cost: Starting from $150 per night

19. Kauai Beach House Hostel

Address: 420 Papaloa Rd, Kapa'a, HI 96746

Cost: Starting from $50 per night (dormitory-style)

20. Tip Top Motel

Address: 3173 Akahi St, Lihue, HI 96766

Cost: Starting from $100 per night

Choosing the correct lodging may drastically affect your whole experience on the lovely island of Kauai. Whether you like the opulent comfort of five-star resorts, the intimacy of a bed & breakfast, or the affordability of budget-friendly choices, Kauai has something to offer every tourist.

Consider your budget, travel style, and preferred location carefully when picking your hotel, and book early to acquire the best possibilities. With a variety of lodgings to select from, you can be confident that your time on the Garden Isle will be memorable and lovely.

Read reviews and reach out to the hotels directly if you have any questions or special requests. Kauai's top-rated hotels provide great service and facilities, ensuring you have a pleasant and pleasurable stay during your time in paradise. Plan your vacation intelligently, and you'll be well on your way to making wonderful experiences on the picturesque island of Kauai.

Also, when picking hotels in Kauai, consider the location that best meets your trip's tastes. Poipu and Princeville are attractive destinations for individuals wanting a more serene atmosphere and access to gorgeous beaches.

Lihue and Kapaa provide a central position for accessible touring of the island, while Hanalei offers a feeling of isolation and closeness to a spectacular natural landscape.

Additionally, bear in mind that the cost of lodgings might vary depending on criteria such as the season, room type, and the facilities provided by each resort. It's essential to reserve well in advance, particularly during busy travel months, to assure your preferred choice of hotel.

Chapter Six

Gastronomic Delights

Food and Dining in Kauai

Kauai's culinary scene is a fascinating combination of traditional Hawaiian flavours, fresh seafood, and cosmopolitan influences. From scrumptious indigenous delicacies to worldwide gourmet cuisine, the island provides a broad assortment of choices to suit every appetite.

Local Cuisine and Must-Try Dishes

1. Poke

A Hawaiian favorite, Poke is a delightful meal prepared with fresh, cubed raw fish (typically tuna) marinated in soy sauce, sesame oil, seaweed, and other ingredients. Served as an appetizer or a light lunch, it's a must-try for seafood fans. Average cost: $10 - $15 per bowl.

2. Laulau

This traditional Hawaiian cuisine consists of pork, butterfish, or both wrapped in taro leaves and cooked to perfection.

The outcome is a soft and savory delicacy that captures the spirit of local culture. Average cost: $15 - $25 per dish.

3. Loco Moco

A hearty Hawaiian comfort meal, Loco Moco contains a bed of steamed rice topped with a hamburger patty, a fried egg, and flavorful brown gravy. It's a delightful and full dinner that will keep you fueled for your island explorations.

Average cost: $12 - $18 per dish.

4. Kalua Pork

A highlight of Hawaiian luaus, Kalua Pork is cooked in an underground oven called an imu, resulting in delicate, smokey, and luscious pork. Served with traditional sides like poi, it delivers a distinctive taste of Hawaii. Average cost: $15 - $20 for each dish.

5. Haupia

A wonderful coconut milk-based delicacy, Haupia has a smooth and creamy texture, akin to custard. Often served as a pudding or in cake shape, it's a delicious dessert that nicely compliments any meal. Average cost: $5 - $8 per dish.

Best Restaurants and Food Stalls

1. Merriman's Fish House

Located in Poipu, Merriman's Fish House is famous for its farm-to-table approach, serving fresh and responsibly sourced fish with beautiful ocean views.

Address: 2829 Ala Kalanikaumaka St., Poipu.

Average cost: $40 - $70 per person.

2. Red Salt

Situated in the Koa Kea Hotel & Resort in Poipu, Red Salt provides a contemporary dining experience, offering regionally inspired cuisine with a modern touch.

Address: 2251 Poipu Road, Poipu.

Average cost: $35 - $60 per person.

3. Eating House, 1849

Created by Chef Roy Yamaguchi, Eating House 1849 pays respect to Hawaii's unique culinary tradition. This restaurant in Koloa provides a fascinating combination of classic and contemporary food. Address: 2829 Ala Kalanikaumaka St, Koloa. Average cost: $30 - $50 per person.

4. Bar Acuda

A tapas-style restaurant in Hanalei, Bar Acuda provides Mediterranean-inspired meals and an extensive wine selection. It's a fantastic area to relax and enjoy the evening.

Address: 5-5161 Kuhio Hwy., Hanalei.

Average cost: $25 - $45 per person.

5. Hanalei Bread Company

For a fast and excellent snack, visit Hanalei Bread Company, where you can enjoy great sandwiches, pastries, and fresh-baked bread in a delightful environment.

Address: 5-5161 Kuhio Hwy., Hanalei.

Average cost: $10 - $20 per person.

6. Hamura Saimin Stand

A local favorite, Hamura Saimin Stand in Lihue, offers you true Hawaiian saimin, a noodle soup flavored with diverse tastes. It's a real taste of the island's gastronomic history.

Address: 2956 Kress St, Lihue.

Average cost: $8 - $15 for each bowl.

7. Koloa Fish Market

This inconspicuous food shop in Koloa delivers some of the freshest and finest fish on the island. Don't miss their poke bowls and fish dishes.

Address: 5482 Koloa Rd, Koloa

Average cost: $10 - $20 per dish

8. Shrimp Station

Located in Waimea, Shrimp Station is recognized for its delectable garlic shrimp dishes and other seafood treats. Address: 9652 Kaumualii Hwy, Waimea.

Average cost: $15 - $25 for each dish.

9. Tidepools

Situated in the Grand Hyatt Kauai Resort & Spa, Tidepools provides a romantic dining experience surrounded by a lagoon and waterfalls. The menu comprises Pacific Rim cuisine with a focus on seafood.

Address: 1571 Poipu Rd, Poipu.

Average cost: $60 - $100 per person.

10. Duke's Kauai

With a fantastic beachside position in Lihue, Duke's Kauai is named after famed surfer Duke Kahanamoku. Enjoy Hawaiian-inspired meals and live music while taking in spectacular ocean views.

Address: 3610 Rice St., Lihue.

Average cost: $30 - $60 per person.

Dietary Options and Recommendations

Kauai's restaurants are often sympathetic to varied dietary choices and limitations, including vegetarian, vegan, gluten-free, and dairy-free offerings. Most places provide menu items labeled with dietary indications, and the pleasant staff is glad to help with any specific requests or alterations.

For vegetarians and vegans, alternatives, including vegetable stir-fries, salads, fruit platters, and plant-based poke bowls, are frequently available. Additionally, several eateries provide inventive plant-based takes on classic Hawaiian meals.

As you tour Kauai's culinary environment, be sure to sample the local delicacies like Poke, Laulau, Loco Moco, and Kalua Pork for a true experience of Hawaiian culture. The island's greatest restaurants and food stalls provide a choice of eating experiences, from premium seaside dining to informal food truck pleasures.

As you enjoy the culinary pleasures and immerse yourself in the beauty of Kauai, may your voyage be filled with wonderful experiences and treasured memories that will live in your heart long after you say the island goodbye.

Chapter Seven

Top Tourist Attractions and Excursions

Kauai, the Garden Isle of Hawaii, has a multitude of magnificent sites and fascinating excursions for guests to experience. In this chapter, we'll dig into the most stunning spots, guided tours, outdoor excursions, and chances to learn about the island's rich history and culture. As you plan your Kauai vacation, keep in mind the admission costs and safety issues for each place.

Natural Wonders: The Most Beautiful Places in Kauai

Napali Coast: A Majestic Adventure Beyond Imagination

The Napali Coast stands as an awe-inspiring tribute to the raw beauty of nature, a length of shoreline that defies the commonplace and captivates the spirit. It's a location where towering cliffs meet the deep blue of the Pacific, where verdant valleys give way to churning surf, and where an aura of mystery and grandeur envelops every inch of its rough landscape. Whether reached by boat, helicopter, or on foot along the legendary Kalalau Trail, the Napali Coast offers a memorable trip into the heart of one of nature's most spectacular masterpieces.

Boat Cruises: A Sea of Wonders

Embarking on a boat ride around the Napali Coast is like entering a nautical masterpiece. As the cliffs rise steeply from the water's edge, you'll be mesmerized by the sheer majesty of nature's construction. These tours give a front-row scat to thc grandeur, enabling you to observe the interplay of light and shadow on the cliffs' surfaces and, if you're fortunate, catch sight of joyful dolphins dancing in the waters. Costs for such an experience vary from $100 to $200 per person, depending on the cruise's length and facilities.

Helicopter Flights: A Skybound Odyssey

For those seeking a genuinely otherworldly experience, a helicopter trip above the Napali Coast gives a panorama that words can hardly convey. Soaring over the insurmountable cliffs and secret valleys, you'll obtain a vista that few have observed. As you stare upon this wonder of nature from the sky, every shape and every fold of the terrain take on a new depth of beauty. Helicopter trips, albeit a little more of an expenditure, ranging from $250 to $500 per person, are nothing short of a sky-bound voyage that will leave an everlasting impact on your memories.

The Kalalau Trail: A Hiker's Ascent

For brave souls with a predilection for the earthly, the Kalalau Trail provides a thrilling trip that penetrates deep into the heart of the Napali Coast. This trek, however, is not for the faint of heart. With its tough terrain and ever-changing weather conditions, it's a challenge best suited for experienced hikers. The trek rewards those who survive it with views that defy belief and the sensation of having conquered one of nature's most difficult environments.

To go on this path, you'll need a permit, which costs $20 per person for a day excursion or $30 if you wish to camp overnight.

Safety and Considerations: Nature's Majesty, Human Caution

As with any contact with nature's magnificence, safety is vital. The Kalalau Trail, in particular, needs respect and preparedness. It's a path that tests not only your physical prowess but also your preparation for the unexpected. Check weather predictions, consult with park officials, and equip yourself with adequate gear before setting foot on this epic adventure.

When it comes to boat and helicopter experiences, selecting renowned firms with excellent safety records is vital. These trips could lead you to the verge of wonder, but never at the expense of your well-being.

In the end, the Napali Coast isn't simply a destination; it's a trip into the very core of nature's grandeur. Whether you choose to explore it from the depths of the ocean, the heights of the sky, or the rugged paths of the trail, this coastline will etch itself into your memory as a place where the extraordinary becomes reality, where cliffs become cathedrals, and where nature stands as the ultimate artist.

- **Waimea Canyon: The Grand Canyon of the Pacific**

Prepare to be amazed by the spectacular splendor of Waimea Canyon, frequently referred to as the "Grand Canyon of the Pacific." This natural marvel is a remarkable tribute to the majesty of nature's creative talent. Spanning over 10 miles in length and reaching depths of up to 3,600 feet, Waimea Canyon is a natural wonder that encourages investigation and adoration.

Waimea Canyon

Spectacular Panoramas: Driving down Waimea Canyon Drive rewards you with a succession of stunning panoramas that showcase the majesty of the canyon from various perspectives. The vibrant red and orange colors of the canyon walls, mixed with the lush greenery of the surrounding flora, create a visual masterpiece that's nothing short of awe-inspiring. Each viewing position along the route gives a fresh perspective, enabling you to fully grasp the grandeur and complexity of this natural beauty.

Free Access and Self-Guided Exploration: One of the most enticing characteristics of Waimea Canyon is its accessibility. There are no admission fees to access the canyon views, making it a great location for those wanting an amazing experience without breaking the budget. Whether you're a seasoned hiker or a casual sightseer, Waimea Canyon provides routes and overlooks ideal for all levels of exploration. The self-guided nature of your tour provides you with the opportunity to choose your own pace, ensuring you can relish every moment and take the ideal images.

Safety Precautions: As you stand in awe of Waimea Canyon's magnificence, it's vital to emphasize safety. The viewing locations are meant to provide a safe vantage point, but it's necessary to take care. Some areas could be slippery, especially in damp weather. Be cautious to remain inside the prescribed zones and respect any safety measures. Avoid standing too close to the brink of cliffs, particularly during windy weather.

Care for Nature: While touring Waimea Canyon, remember to treat this natural beauty with the greatest care. Leave no evidence of your presence, and ensure that you don't upset the delicate balance of the ecology. Capture memories via your camera lens rather than deleting natural features, so that others may have the same awe-inspiring experience for years to come.

The Grandeur of Waimea Canyon Awaits: Waimea Canyon is more than simply a geological wonder; it's a tribute to the force of natural processes that have molded the Earth's surface over millions of years. From the vivid hues that cover the canyon walls to the lush flora that flourishes inside its depths, every part of Waimea Canyon tells a narrative of geological history and the eternal forces of nature.

As you walk up Waimea Canyon Drive and stand at the viewpoint spots, take a minute to appreciate the overwhelming magnitude and beauty that surround you. The "Grand Canyon of the Pacific" stands as a tribute to the marvelous intricacy of our world, asking you to explore, enjoy, and marvel at the incredible creation that is Waimea Canyon. Just remember to walk cautiously, prioritize safety, and treasure the memories you'll build among this natural magnificence.

- **Hanalei Bay: A Tranquil Oasis on Kauai's North Shore**

Nestled along Kauai's gorgeous North Shore, Hanalei Bay is a quiet refuge of natural beauty and enticing waters. This magnificent beach is not only a destination; it's an experience that encompasses the essence of Hawaii's charm. With its tranquil ambience, broad crescent-shaped beach, and lush surroundings, Hanalei Bay is a jewel that captivates travelers with its timeless beauty.

Beach Bliss and Activities

Hanalei Bay provides a typical beach experience, providing an exquisite location for leisure and entertainment. The golden sands extend beautifully down the coast, beckoning beachgoers to lay their towels, soak up the sun, and enjoy the rhythmic sound of waves caressing against the shore. Swimming in the tranquil waters is a treat, and the bay's moderate slope guarantees a comfortable transition into deeper waters.

Beach Bliss

For those seeking more daring hobbies, Hanalei Bay offers a range of water sports. Kayaking and stand-up paddleboarding are popular activities that enable you to see the bay from a fresh viewpoint. The bay's mild waves are also suitable for newbie surfers anxious to catch their first wave.

Safety and Considerations

While Hanalei Bay is recognized for its tranquil seas, it's vital to practice care and be cognizant of safety standards. The ocean's conditions may fluctuate, and although swimming is typically safe, it's crucial to pay attention to surf conditions and respect any posted cautions. It's essential to speak with local lifeguards or beach specialists who can give real-time information regarding currents and possible risks.

Surfing and local culture

Hanalei Bay maintains a particular place in the hearts of both inhabitants and tourists, and its importance goes beyond its physical beauty. The bay has gained its reputation as a surfing sanctuary, inviting surfers from across the globe to ride its legendary waves. The bay's waves appeal to a variety of ability levels, making it a perfect site for both novices and expert surfers to enjoy the sport.

Beyond its natural allure, Hanalei Bay is a dynamic component of the local culture. The surrounding village of Hanalei radiates a laid-back appeal, with its modest boutiques, art galleries, and pleasant eateries adding to the area's welcome vibe. Engaging with the local people and immersing yourself in the distinct culture gives an added depth of authenticity to your Hanalei Bay experience.

Hanalei Bay isn't simply a destination; it's a voyage into a world of peace, beauty, and adventure. From its sun-kissed shoreline and gentle waves to the colorful local culture that surrounds it, the bay represents the character of Kauai's North Shore. Whether you're seeking a tranquil day of leisure or an intense day of water sports, Hanalei Bay greets you with open arms, encouraging you to make memories that will live in your heart long after you've left its enchanted embrace.

- **Discover the beauty of the Wailua River and Falls**

Nestled on the island of Kauai sits a beautiful natural marvel that calls guests to go on an extraordinary journey—the famed Wailua River and Falls. This stunning scene is a monument to Kauai's immense beauty, presenting a combination of calm streams, lush greenery, and the dramatic Wailua Falls. Whether you prefer to explore via guided boat excursions or on your own with rental kayaks, this chapter will lead you through the magical experience of the Wailua River.

Exploring the Wailua River: Guided Boat Tours and Kayak Adventures

The Wailua River is a treasure trove of natural beauty and cultural value. There are two popular ways to immerse oneself in its charm: guided boat cruises and kayak expeditions.

Guided Boat Tours: Dive into the heart of Wailua's magic by selecting a guided boat excursion. Cruise down the winding river, surrounded by gorgeous vistas that have charmed travelers for years. Guided boat trips give not only a pleasant and gorgeous ride but also interesting commentary from local guides, who convey the rich history and cultural importance of the region. As you float around, keep an eye out for historic

Hawaiian temples and monuments that still survive as symbols of the island's past.

Kayak Adventures: For those wanting a more hands-on and personal relationship with the river, renting kayaks is an attractive choice. Paddle at your own speed, letting the serene beat of the river lead you through the bright splendor of Wailua. As you travel the river, you'll see secluded coves, beautiful flora, and possibly even observe local species. The excursion becomes a personal investigation of the river's nooks and crannies, providing you with a unique view of this natural marvel.

Cost and logistics

Guided boat trips: The cost of guided boat trips varies from around $30 to $80 per person, depending on the length and particular elements of the tour. While some excursions concentrate on the river's natural beauty, others may combine visits to historical sites or cultural events, improving the whole experience.

Kayak Rentals: To begin on a kayak expedition, you should anticipate paying roughly $50 to $100 per day for kayak rentals. It's recommended to arrange rentals from trusted and well-regarded organizations, guaranteeing you obtain excellent equipment and the required safety instructions.

Admission Fees: Unlike many tourist locations, there are no admission fees necessary to view Wailua Falls. This accessibility enables tourists to fully enjoy the charm of the falls without financial limitations.

Safety Considerations

While both guided boat trips and kayak expeditions offer memorable experiences, safety should always be a concern. For kayak adventures, find a trustworthy rental firm that provides well-maintained equipment and safety procedures. Be aware of river conditions and water levels, particularly if you're not an experienced kayaker. During boat tours, observe the safety guidelines issued by your expert guides.

As you commence your trek down the Wailua River, take a minute to enjoy the calm and beauty that surrounds you. Whether you're floating along on a guided boat or paddling your own kayak, the Wailua River and Falls guarantee an unforgettable interaction with nature's beauty and the rich history of Kauai.

- **Spouting Horn: Witness Nature's Spectacle**

In the enchanting region of Kauai, where nature's creative talent is on full display, lies the Spouting Horn, a spectacular natural phenomenon near the tranquil Poipu Beach. This magnificent blowhole is an aquatic masterpiece, affording visitors a breathtaking aquatic display that never fails to inspire astonishment.

The Aquatic Melody: As waves crash across the rocky beach, the Spouting Horn orchestrates a beautiful melody. Through an old lava tube that conducts ocean water, the waves' power forces water through a tiny hole in the lava rock, causing it to explode into a spectacular plume that may reach incredible heights. This beautiful spectacle is complemented by a loud hissing sound, like a symphony of nature itself.

Accessibility and Cost: Nature's beauty at Spouting Horn is available for everybody to marvel at. There are no entry costs to witness this magnificence. The facility is readily accessible, with a short walk from the parking lot to the viewing platforms. As you approach the edge, the suspense increases, and the sheer strength of the ocean can be felt in each spray that showers your skin.

Safety First: While the appeal of getting up close to this aquatic beauty is great, safety is crucial. The viewing platforms are purposefully positioned to provide a good vantage point while keeping tourists at a safe distance. Remember, nature's performance is unexpected, and the water's power might be strong. Remaining on authorized platforms guarantees you can experience the show without sacrificing your safety.

Tips for a thrilling experience
To make the most of your visit to Spouting Horn:

Timing is key. Plan your visit at high tide for the most stunning spectacle, as the waves' force is at its highest.

Capturing the Moment: Have your camera ready to record the awe-inspiring moment when the water pours through the blowhole, producing a stunning spray against the background of the ocean.

Embrace the surroundings: The sweeping ocean panoramas and the natural beauty of the surrounding region are a treat to see. Take some time to absorb the gorgeous environment.

Respect Nature: As with other natural attractions, it's crucial to handle the environment with care and respect. Avoid trash and remain on authorized routes to conserve the sensitive habitat.

Awe and wonder Await: Visiting Spouting Horn is a voyage into the heart of Kauai's natural majesty. As you experience the sea's raw strength transformed into a symphony of water and music, you'll be reminded of the tremendous forces that created our planet. The dance of waves, the explosion of water, and the harmonic hiss of nature create a sensory experience that will be carved into your mind.

So, stroll onto the observation platforms, let the mist contact your skin, and experience the energy of the ocean as it performs its aquatic masterpiece at Spouting Horn. In every spray, you'll discover a connection to the vast force of nature and a profound respect for the beauty that lives in even the most unexpected corners of the globe.

Recommended Time to Visit Each Location

- Na Pali Coast: The best time to visit the Na Pali Coast is during the summer months, from May to September. During this month, the ocean conditions are calmer, allowing for smoother boat excursions and improved visibility for helicopter tours. Hiking is also more doable, but be cautious to verify weather conditions and trail closures.

- Waimea Canyon: Waimea Canyon may be visited year-round, however, the views are frequently crisper during the dry months of April to October. However, going during the wetter months (November to March) might reward you with brilliant green landscapes and more magnificent waterfalls.

- Hanalei Bay: The lovely Hanalei Bay is appealing year-round. The summer months provide calmer waves, which are excellent for swimming and water activities. Winter offers stronger waves, attracting surfers from across the globe. Choose your activities depending on the season.

- Wailua Falls: These falls run year-round; however, they may be more spectacular during times of high rainfall. For the finest experience, come during the wetter months when the falls are at their fullest.

- Poipu Beach: Poipu Beach is a popular location throughout the year, giving superb beach conditions and snorkeling chances throughout the summer. It's also a good place for whale-watching from November to April.

- Kalalau route: The Kalalau Trail is available year-round, but it's vital to verify weather and route conditions before beginning on this tough walk. The dry months of May through September are often preferred for more stable trail conditions.

- Limahuli Garden and Preserve: This garden is a great site to explore year-round. However, the scenery is frequently lushest during the wetter months from November through March.

How to Get to Kauai from Major Continents

From North America (US Mainland)

- The most popular method to reach Kauai from the US mainland is by flying. Many major airlines provide direct flights to Lihue Airport (LIH) from destinations including Los Angeles,

San Francisco, Seattle, and Denver. Flight lengths normally vary from 5 to 7 hours, depending on your departure city.

From Europe (UK)

- There are no direct flights from the UK to Kauai, so passengers will need to connect via major US cities like Los Angeles, San Francisco, or Seattle. The overall journey duration, including layovers, might vary but normally takes roughly 15 to 20 hours.

From Asia (Japan, China, South Korea, etc.)

- Several airlines operate direct flights from major Asian cities to Honolulu International Airport (HNL) on Oahu. From there, passengers may take a short inter-island flight to Lihue Airport on Kauai. The overall journey duration, including the inter-island flight, is normally approximately 10 to 12 hours.

From Australia and New Zealand:

- tourists from Australia and New Zealand may reach Kauai through connecting flights via major US cities like Los Angeles or Honolulu. The overall trip duration might vary, depending on layovers, but normally takes from 12 to 16 hours.

As you plan your visit to Kauai, be sure to book your flights and lodgings well in advance, particularly during high tourist seasons. Whether you're seeking beautiful panoramas, thrilling treks, or a calm beach escape, Kauai promises to be a place that will surpass your expectations and leave you with wonderful memories.

Guided Tours and Activities

1. Helicopter Tours

Helicopter rides give a unique view of Kauai's natural beauty. Prices might vary depending on the trip length and facilities supplied by various operators. It's crucial to hire an FAA-certified operator with experienced pilots.

Safety: Helicopter excursions are typically safe, but ensure you follow all safety recommendations offered by the operator. Keep in mind that helicopters may be loud, so wear ear protection.

2. Boat Tours and Snorkeling

Boat cruises along the Napali Coast or to Niihau normally cost from $100 to $200 per person. Snorkeling trips may charge an extra fee for gear rental.

Safety: Opt for boat cruises with skilled crew members that emphasize passenger safety. Follow all safety recommendations while snorkeling activities and use suitable snorkeling gear.

3. Movie Tours

Movie excursions give an amazing chance to explore classic shooting sites around Kauai. Prices might vary dependent on the time and scope of regions covered.

Safety: Movie tours entail little physical danger, but always follow the guide's directions and respect the environment throughout the trip.

4. Sunset Cruises

Sunset cruises are a tranquil way to see the beauty of Kauai's shoreline throughout the sunset. Prices may vary from $50 to $150 per person.

Safety: Sunset cruises are typically safe, but be careful of motion sickness, particularly if you're prone to seasickness. Stay inside the specified places on the boat for your safety.

Outdoor Adventures: Hiking, Water Sports, and More

1. Kalalau Trail

Hiking the Kalalau Trail requires a permit, which costs $20 per person for a day trip or $30 for an overnight stay.

Only experienced hikers should try this tough trek, which runs 11 miles one way.

Safety: The Kalalau Trail is rough and may be perilous in some spots. Ensure you are physically healthy, and well-prepared with adequate hiking gear, and verify weather conditions before beginning this adventure.

2. Snorkeling and Scuba Diving

While snorkeling is often free at many beaches, renting snorkeling gear might cost roughly $10 to $20 per day. For scuba diving, organized excursions with equipment rental normally range from $100 to $150 per person.

Safety: Always snorkel and scuba dive with a companion and keep within your ability level. Follow the recommendations suggested by your instructor during scuba diving activities.

3. Kayaking and Stand-Up Paddleboarding

Kayak rentals may cost from $50 to $100 per day, while stand-up paddleboard rentals are comparable in price. Guided kayak trips may cost from $100 to $200 per person.

Safety: Choose a kayak excursion that meets your skill level and experience. Wear life jackets and observe safety rules supplied by rental providers.

4. Ziplining

Ziplining experiences normally cost from $100 to $150 per person, depending on the number of lines and extra attractions.

Safety: Opt for ziplining trips done by trained operators with contemporary equipment and adequate safety precautions.

Exploring Kauai's Culture and History

1. Kauai Museum

Immersing in the Island's History and Culture

When you walk inside the Kauai Museum, you're not simply entering a structure; you're beginning a thrilling journey through the heart and spirit of the island. Situated in the lovely village of

Lihue, this cultural treasure trove serves as a custodian of Kauai's rich history, customs, and legacy. Beyond its doors lies a tapestry created from the history of the island's people, their difficulties and successes, and the undying spirit that distinguishes Kauai.

Preserving the Past, Inspiring the Future

As you tour the museum's halls, you'll be welcomed into an immersive experience that brings the past to life. From the early Hawaiians' arrival to the echoes of plantation life, the Kauai Museum's displays chronicle the island's growth through the centuries. The antiques, images, and interactive exhibits serve as windows to a period when canoes sailed down the coastlines, sugarcane fields swung in the breeze, and traditions were handed down from generation to generation.

A Small Price for a Significant Impact

The Kauai Museum's aim extends beyond merely exhibiting history; it's about conserving it. The entry price, typically $15 per adult, acts as an investment in the protection of Hawaiian culture. It supports the museum's continuous work to conserve and repair items, provide educational programs, and undertake research that sheds light on Kauai's varied history.

Safety and Respect: A Shared Responsibility

While reveling in the museum's displays, it's crucial to enjoy your experience properly. The island's legacy is not only recorded inside these walls but also lives within the hearts of its inhabitants. To respect this relationship, obey any instructions or limits offered by the museum employees. By doing so, you contribute to the preservation of the displays for future generations to cherish.

A Window to Understanding

The Kauai Museum isn't simply a collection of antiques; it's a living tribute to the island's character. It's a site where the tales of chiefs, fishermen, missionaries, and plantation laborers collide, generating the colorful tapestry that is Kauai's history. As you walk through the displays, you'll obtain a greater knowledge of the island's beginnings, its hardships, and its resilience.

So, step inside the Kauai Museum and let its treasures take you through time. Let the whispers of the past lead you as you travel its hallways, providing a vivid picture of Kauai's growth. And when you go, consider that your visit has contributed not just to your personal learning but to the preservation of an island's soul. Your entry price isn't only a transaction; it's an investment in the continuous celebration of Kauai's history and the maintenance of its culture.

Limahuli Garden & Preserve: A Natural Haven of Beauty and Conservation

Nestled on the north coast of Kauai, the Limahuli Garden & Preserve serves as a tribute to the island's incredible biodiversity and the hard work of conservationists. This beautiful oasis provides visitors a chance to immerse themselves in a stunning tapestry of native Hawaiian flora while helping to preserve this vulnerable environment.

A Priceless Experience with a Purpose

At an entry fee of around $20 per adult, a visit to Limahuli Garden is not just a casual walk through magnificent landscapes; it's an investment in the future of Kauai's unique environment.

The monies collected from the registration fees serve a key role in financing ongoing conservation projects. By touring the garden, you become a participant in a greater endeavor to safeguard the very spirit of the Garden Isle.

Conservation in the Heart of Limahuli

The Garden and Preserve's principal aim is to restore and conserve native Hawaiian plants, many of which are endangered due to invasive species and habitat degradation. By visiting Limahuli, you actively support these conservation activities. The garden acts as a living laboratory, where scientists work diligently to propagate and reintroduce vulnerable species, guaranteeing their existence for years to come.

Walking Lightly on Nature's Canvas

As you wander through Limahuli's lovely paths, it's vital to observe the garden's standards to safeguard the conservation of its fragile flora and animals. Staying on authorized paths not only assures your safety but also saves the sensitive ecology from unexpected impacts. By observing these instructions, you become an eco-conscious visitor, helping to preserve Kauai's natural legacy.

An Educational Journey

Limahuli Garden provides more than simply spectacular beauty; it's an educational excursion into the realm of Hawaiian ethnobotany, history, and culture. Along the route, you'll discover instructive signage that offers insight on the importance of numerous plants to Hawaiian custom and everyday life. This interactive experience links you with the underlying storylines that have defined Kauai's cultural environment.

A Lasting Impact

As you explore rare species and beautiful petals, you'll surely leave Limahuli Garden with more than just images. You'll take with you a feeling of purpose, knowing that your visit has helped to preserve a unique environment. By supporting Limahuli's conservation efforts, you're playing an active part in ensuring that Kauai's natural treasures continue to thrive for decades to come.

In summation, the Limahuli Garden and Preserve provides not only a visual feast of beauty but a meaningful connection to Kauai's natural history. Your entry charge transcends the function of a ticket; it becomes a contribution to the island's conservation heritage. By walking softly and adopting the garden's principles, you become a custodian of this fragile environment. As you explore, learn, and enjoy the complex tapestry of life that Limahuli provides, you'll exit with a feeling of contentment, knowing that your visit has left a lasting influence on the Garden Isle.

Smith's Tropical Paradise Luau: A Cultural Feast of Flavor and Entertainment

When it comes to witnessing the vivid tapestry of Hawaiian culture while enjoying an evening of riveting entertainment, Smith's Tropical Paradise Luau stands out as an outstanding must-visit site on the island of Kauai. This isn't just a dinner; it's a sensory voyage into the heart of Hawaiian customs, all set against the gorgeous background of Kauai's amazing natural splendor.

A Culinary and Cultural Extravaganza: Smith's Tropical Paradise Luau is more than simply a wonderful supper; it's a feast for the senses. As you experience the wonderful selection of Hawaiian and Polynesian foods, each mouthful becomes a celebration of flavors and a gastronomic tour of the area. From juicy kalua pig, slow-roasted to perfection, to fresh seafood and tropical fruits bursting with freshness, every dish is a tribute to the island's rich culinary tradition.

Immersive Cultural Experience: But the Luau experience at Smith's is considerably more than simply a gastronomic feast. It's an immersion into the heart and spirit of Hawaiian culture. From the minute you arrive, you're welcomed with a traditional lei, a mark of welcome and friendliness. As you explore the beautiful surroundings, you'll find yourself attracted by the tales, dances, and songs that have been handed down through centuries.

Captivating culture: The evening comes alive with a lively and genuine presentation of Polynesian and Hawaiian culture. The rhythmic sound of drums and the elegant motions of hula dancers take you to a realm where history and tales are represented through every action. You'll see the fascinating fire dance, a sight that puts you in awe of the artists' ability and daring.

Environment amidst natural splendor: One of the distinguishing elements that sets Smith's Luau apart is its gorgeous environment. The gorgeous tropical gardens and peaceful seas offer the ideal background for this cultural spectacular. As the sun sets and the sky changes into a canvas of vivid colors, you'll find yourself surrounded by a symphony of colors that elegantly complement the performances and the mood.

A Uniquely Enriching Experience: Smith's Tropical Paradise Luau is more than an event; it's a journey that links you with the soul of Hawaii. It's an opportunity to get insight into the island's traditions, to experience the power of dance and storytelling, and to join in the wonderful spirit of aloha that binds natives and tourists alike. It's a reminder that beyond its magnificent surroundings, Hawaii's genuine richness rests in its culture and people.

Make reservations early. As one of Kauai's most sought-after experiences, Smith's Luau tends to fill up fast, particularly during high tourism seasons. To guarantee you secure your seat at this cultural feast of taste and fun, it's essential to make reservations well in advance.

An Unforgettable Memory: Smith's Tropical Paradise Luau offers an evening that exceeds the ordinary. It's an event that sticks in your mind long after the final note of music has faded and the last dance has concluded. Whether you're a solitary traveler, a couple seeking romance, or a family searching for a meaningful and engaging experience, our luau assures an amazing evening of cultural immersion, gastronomic indulgence, and pure enchantment amongst the natural beauties of Kauai.

Cultural Immersion

At Smith's Tropical Paradise Luau, guests get the chance to dig deep into the traditions and customs of Hawaii. The luau opens with a heartfelt aloha welcome, setting the tone for an evening packed with music, dancing, and tales that represent the island's rich tradition. Traditional performances, like hula dances and Polynesian fire dancing, transport tourists to a bygone era, enabling them to connect with the essence of the islands.

The Feast

Central to the luau experience is the feast—a tempting assortment of genuine Hawaiian foods that demonstrate the island's culinary diversity. From kalua pig, slow-cooked in an imu (subterranean oven), to fresh fish, tropical fruits, and poi (a traditional Hawaiian dish prepared from taro root), the menu is a celebration of local cuisine. The mix of tastes and fragrances produces an amazing eating experience that pays tribute to both the island's heritage and its present-day gourmet offerings.

Cost and Value

The cost of attending a luau at Smith's Tropical Paradise normally varies from $100 to $150 per adult, which includes entry to the feast and the colorful entertainment. While this could look like an investment, it's crucial to examine the entire value of the experience. Beyond the exquisite cuisine, the luau gives a true peek into Hawaiian culture that is frequently difficult to discover elsewhere. It's a chance to acquire insight into the tales, music, and dance that have defined the island's identity.

Safety Considerations

Luau locations, like Smith's Tropical Paradise, stress the safety and well-being of their visitors. Generally, luau gatherings are considered safe venues for people to enjoy the festivities. However, like with any event, it's recommended to be aware of your surroundings and comply with any safety precautions supplied by the hosts. Pay attention to announcements and take note of any safety advice offered throughout the luau.

Creating lasting memories

A visit to Smith's Tropical Paradise Luau is more than simply a dinner; it's a chance to make lasting memories and friendships. As you experience the delicacies of Hawaii, surrounded by the island's natural beauty and the rhythmic rhythms of traditional music, you'll find yourself carried away in the enchantment of the moment. It's an opportunity to not only enjoy a feast for the senses but to also get a greater grasp of Kauai's diverse cultural tapestry.

So, if you're looking for an evening of cultural immersion, gastronomic pleasures, and energetic entertainment, don't miss out on the opportunity to join Smith's Tropical Paradise Luau. Whether you're a solitary traveler, a couple on a romantic holiday, or a family wanting to enjoy a unique experience, the luau guarantees an exquisite evening that celebrates the heart and spirit of Kauai.

Hawaiian Heiau (Temples)

Exploring Hawaiian Heiau: Unveiling Kauai's Spiritual Heritage

Delve into the depths of Kauai's spiritual past by going on a visit to its traditional Hawaiian heiau (temples). These historic ruins, tucked within the island's stunning landscapes, give a unique chance to connect with the island's history and acquire insights into its cultural and spiritual importance. As you visit these hallowed lands, you'll encounter a tremendous feeling of respect and wonder that still resonates today.

A Glimpse at Ancient Traditions

Hawaiian heiau are more than simply architectural buildings; they are expressions of the island's rich cultural legacy. These temples functioned as sites of worship, ceremonies, and social meetings for the island's local inhabitants. Each heiau has its own specific function, whether it is for giving prayers to deities, seeking advice from ancestors, or commemorating noteworthy celestial occurrences. By visiting these locations, you're taken back in time to an age when faith was intimately intertwined with the fabric of everyday life.

Connecting with the Divine and Natural

One of the noteworthy qualities of these heiau is their connection to the natural environment. Many of them are intentionally positioned to correspond with astronomical occurrences, like solstices and equinoxes, highlighting the intimate bond between the Hawaiian people and the land, sea, and sky. The tranquility of these areas inspires visitors to halt, ponder, and interact with the energy of their surroundings, generating a feeling of oneness with both the sacred and the natural.

Respecting Sacred Spaces

While discovering these heiau is a gift, it comes with the duty to respect their holiness. It's vital to approach these places with respect, humility, and a thorough awareness of their value. Many heiau are placed in public locations and may be freely visited. However, there are criteria to comply with in order to maintain the preservation of these hallowed places:

Do Not Disturb: Refrain from touching or removing any things inside the house. These objects possess cultural and spiritual value and should be preserved undisturbed.

Observe notifications and cautions: Pay heed to any signs or notifications placed near the heiau. Some locations may have unique regulations or limitations in place to safeguard both visitors and the facility itself.

Environmental Stewardship: Take care to avoid hurting the natural environment when visiting these hallowed locations. Stick to approved trails and avoid harming the surrounding vegetation and creatures.

A Soothing Harmony with the Past

Visiting Hawaiian Heiau on Kauai is not simply a physical excursion; it's a spiritual and emotional one. As you stand inside the stone walls that have weathered the test of time, you're asked to connect with the mana (spiritual energy) of the land and pay tribute to the island's ancestors.

The tranquility that envelops these monuments serves as a reminder of the continuity of traditions and the ongoing link between the past and the present.

Exploring Kauai's historic heiau is an enlightening experience that enables you to tread in the footsteps of ancient Hawaiians, gaining insight into their spiritual rituals and great appreciation for the natural environment. By approaching these holy places with respect and humility, you may embark on a trip that not only links you with the island's history but also leaves you with a deep feeling of wonder and thankfulness for the cultural riches maintained within Kauai's landscapes.

Map Directions

1. Napali Coast: To visit the Napali Coast by boat, proceed to the North Shore of Kauai, where cruises leave from the ports at Hanalei or Port Allen. Helicopter rides depart from Lihue Airport. If you want to walk the Kalalau Trail, the trailhead is situated at the end of Highway 56 near Ke'e Beach.

2. Waimea Canyon: Waimea Canyon is situated on the western edge of Kauai. Drive down Waimea Canyon Drive (Highway 550) from Waimea Town to visit the many viewpoint sites and trails.

3. Hanalei Bay: Hanalei Bay is located on the North Shore of Kauai, accessible from Hanalei Town. Follow Highway 560 to reach the Bay Area.

4. Wailua River and Falls: The Wailua River is readily accessible from Highway 56. For guided boat cruises, proceed to Wailua Marina. To visit Wailua Falls, use Mahalo Road off Highway 56.

5. Spouting Horn: Spouting Horn is situated along Lawa'i Road in Poipu. From the main Poipu Road, follow the signs to Spouting Horn Park.

Safety Considerations

1. Always check the weather and ocean conditions before going on any outdoor activities, particularly those involving water.

2. Follow all safety standards and instructions supplied by trip organizers and guides.

3. Stay on established routes and pathways when hiking to prevent getting lost or damaging precious ecosystems.

4. Respect cultural and historical landmarks by complying to any restrictions and standards issued by local authorities.

5. Be cognizant of your physical ability and pick activities that match your skill level and fitness.

6. Carry vital supplies such as sunscreen, water, bug repellant, and any required prescriptions for outdoor activities.

7. Be careful of your surroundings and animals, particularly while trekking in rural locations.

8. If indulging in water activities, use adequate safety gear such as life jackets and snorkeling fins.

Kauai's top tourist sites and excursions give you an unequaled chance to immerse yourself in the island's natural beauty and cultural legacy. From the magnificent Napali Coast to the abundant aquatic life under the water, Kauai delivers a broad assortment of experiences for every tourist. While planning your trips, remember to consider admission costs and safety measures, and respect the local environment and culture. By doing so, you may fully experience the charms of Kauai while assuring a safe and pleasurable vacation on the Garden Isle. Enjoy your adventures, and may your stay on Kauai be filled with treasured moments and lasting memories.

Chapter Eight

Travel Costs and Budgeting

When planning a trip to Kauai, understanding the travel costs and budgeting appropriately is essential to ensuring a smooth and enjoyable experience on the Garden Isle. This chapter will provide you with in-depth knowledge and insights into estimating travel expenses, money-saving tips and deals, and effective strategies for managing your budget while exploring Kauai's beauty and attractions.

Estimating Travel Expenses

Flights and Transportation: The major expense for most travelers to Kauai is the cost of flights and transportation. The airfare to Kauai can vary significantly based on the time of year, booking in advance, and departure city. It's advisable to use flight comparison websites to find the best deals. Additionally, consider signing up for fare alerts to stay updated on any price drops.

Accommodation: Kauai offers a wide range of accommodation options, from luxury resorts to budget-friendly guesthouses.

Prices will vary based on the location, amenities, and time of year. Research various lodging options and book well in advance to secure better rates. Alternatively, consider staying in vacation rentals or local B&Bs for a more authentic experience and potential cost savings.

Food and Dining: Dining expenses can add up quickly, especially if you eat at high-end restaurants regularly. While enjoying local cuisine is a must, it's also beneficial to explore affordable eateries, food trucks, and farmers' markets. You can save money by having a mix of restaurant meals and self-catering with grocery purchases. Save between $50-$100 daily, depending on your choices of feeling

Activities and Tours: Kauai offers a plethora of exciting activities and tours, ranging from helicopter rides over scenic landscapes to snorkeling adventures in pristine waters. Research the activities you want to experience, compare prices, and consider booking in advance to secure discounts and avoid last-minute price hikes.

Miscellaneous Expenses: Be sure to budget for miscellaneous expenses like souvenirs, tips, parking fees, and any additional attractions or experiences that may catch your interest during your visit.

Money-Saving Tips and Deals

Travel During Off-Peak Seasons: The best way to save on travel expenses to Kauai is by visiting during the off-peak seasons.

Prices for accommodation, flights, and tours tend to be lower, and you'll also encounter fewer crowds, allowing for a more peaceful and intimate experience of the island.

Flexibility with Travel Dates: If your travel dates are flexible, use fare comparison tools to find the cheapest days to fly. Flying on weekdays or during less popular travel periods can lead to significant savings.

Package Deals and Bundles: Consider purchasing travel packages that combine flights, accommodations, and activities. Many travel agencies and websites offer bundled deals that can save you money compared to booking each component separately.

Discount Cards and Passes: Look for attraction passes or discount cards that offer access to multiple activities and sights at a reduced rate. These passes often include popular attractions and can be an excellent way to save on entrance fees.

Public Transportation and Carpooling: Utilize public transportation, such as buses or shuttles, to get around the island, especially for shorter distances. Carpooling with fellow travelers or joining group tours can also help split costs.

Managing Your Budget While on Kauai

- Create a Detailed Itinerary: Plan your activities and allocate a budget for each day to stay on track. Having a well-structured itinerary will help you avoid impulse spending and make the most of your time on the island

- Track Expenses: Keep track of your spending throughout your trip. There are numerous budgeting apps available that can help you monitor your expenses and identify areas where you can cut back.

- Cook Your Own Meals: Consider staying in accommodations with kitchen facilities and preparing some of your meals. Shopping at local grocery stores and markets can be an enjoyable experience and help you save on dining costs.

- Free and Low-Cost Activities: Kauai offers several free and low-cost activities, such as hiking trails, beach days, and exploring charming towns. Embrace these opportunities to experience the island without breaking the bank.
- Set Aside a Contingency Fund: Unexpected expenses can arise during your travels. Set aside a contingency fund to cover emergencies, so you don't have to dip into your planned budget.

Budgeting for your trip to Kauai is crucial to ensuring you have a stress-free and memorable experience without overspending. By estimating your travel expenses, using money-saving tips and deals, and managing your budget effectively, you can fully immerse yourself in the wonders of Kauai while keeping your finances in check. Remember, with thoughtful planning and smart spending, your journey to the Garden Isle will be a journey of a lifetime.

Chapter Nine

Safety Tips for Traveling in Kauai

Kauai, with its breathtaking landscapes and captivating attractions, is a paradise for travelers. However, like any other travel destination, it's essential to prioritize safety during your visit. This chapter provides in-depth safety guidelines and precautions for your journey to the Garden Isle, ensuring you have a secure and enjoyable experience.

General Safety Guidelines

a. Stay Informed: Before embarking on your Kauai adventure, familiarize yourself with the local laws, customs, and regulations. Stay updated on weather conditions, potential hazards, and any travel advisories issued by official authorities.

b. Travel Insurance: Purchase comprehensive travel insurance that covers medical emergencies, trip cancellations, and any unforeseen incidents. Ensure your policy includes outdoor activities and adventure sports if you plan to indulge in them.

c. Emergency Contacts: Program emergency numbers into your phone and keep a list of essential contacts, including local hospitals, police stations, and your country's embassy or consulate, in case of any emergencies.

d. Safe Storage: Use hotel safes or secure storage options to safeguard your valuables, such as passports, cash, and electronics. When exploring, avoid displaying expensive items openly.

e. Photography Etiquette: While capturing memories, be respectful of local customs and avoid taking pictures of sacred places, private properties, or individuals without their permission.

f. Traveling Solo: If you're traveling alone, inform someone back home about your itinerary and check in regularly. Stay in well-populated areas and avoid isolated locations during the night.

g. Cultural Sensitivity: Embrace and respect the local culture. Learn basic phrases in the Hawaiian language, follow appropriate dress codes for sacred sites, and avoid behaviors that might offend the locals.

Outdoor Safety and Precautions

a. Hiking Preparations: Kauai boasts stunning hiking trails, but preparation is crucial. Research your chosen trail, assess your fitness level, and bring adequate supplies, including water, snacks, a map, and a first-aid kit.

b. Weather Awareness: Kauai's weather can be unpredictable. Check weather forecasts before venturing out and be prepared for sudden changes. Dress in layers to adapt to varying temperatures.

c. Flash Floods: Kauai is susceptible to flash floods, especially in certain areas. Never attempt to cross flooded roads or streams. Heed warning signs, and if caught in a flash flood, seek higher ground immediately.

d. Wildlife Encounters: While exploring Kauai's lush wilderness, you may encounter native wildlife. Maintain a safe distance from animals, especially those with young, and refrain from feeding them.

e. Sun Protection: The Hawaiian sun can be intense. Wear sunscreen with high SPF, a wide-brimmed hat, sunglasses, and lightweight, protective clothing to shield yourself from harmful UV rays.

f. Leave No Trace: Practise responsible tourism by leaving no trace of your presence. Respect nature by not littering, damaging vegetation, or disturbing wildlife.

g. Terrain Caution: Be cautious on uneven terrain, slippery rocks, and cliff edges. Pay attention to warning signs and barriers at viewpoints for your safety.

Beach Safety and Ocean Awareness

a. Know Your Limitations: While Kauai offers beautiful beaches and ideal conditions for various water activities, assess your swimming abilities honestly. If unsure, stick to shallow waters.

b. Rip Currents: Kauai's beaches can experience strong rip currents. Always swim in areas with lifeguards present and adhere to their instructions. If caught in a rip current, swim parallel to the shore until free, then swim back.

c. High Surf: During high surf advisories, avoid entering the water, especially near rocky shorelines or cliffs, as waves can be dangerous and unpredictable.

d. Snorkeling Safety: If snorkeling, do so in designated snorkeling spots with calm waters and abundant marine life.

Avoid touching or stepping on coral reefs to preserve the fragile ecosystem.

e. Jellyfish and Marine Stingers: Occasionally, jellyfish and other marine stingers may be present in the waters around Kauai. Familiarize yourself with their appearance and follow local advice if stung.

f. Boating Safety: If engaging in boating or water sports, wear life jackets and follow all safety guidelines. Check weather conditions and tides before heading out.

g. Sunset Safety: Kauai's sunsets are a sight to behold, but never turn your back on the ocean during sunset. Rogue waves can occur and catch you off guard.

Kauai is a destination filled with awe-inspiring experiences and unforgettable adventures. By adhering to these safety tips and precautions, you can fully immerse yourself in the island's beauty while ensuring your well-being throughout your journey. Always prioritize safety, and let the spirit of aloha guide you on your remarkable Kauai exploration.

Chapter Ten

Best Time to Visit Kauai

Kauai's stunning natural beauty and diverse landscapes make it a year-round destination, but choosing the best time to visit can significantly enhance your experience on the Garden Isle. In this chapter, we will provide you with an in-depth analysis of Kauai's weather and climate, the distinction between peak and off-season travel, and a comprehensive list of special events and festivals. Additionally, we will delve into climate-specific activities and offer a detailed breakdown of the wet and dry seasons.

Weather and Climate

Kauai enjoys a tropical climate, characterized by warm temperatures, trade winds, and occasional rain showers. The island experiences two primary seasons: the dry season (Kauwela) and the wet season (Ho'ilo). Understanding the island's climate patterns will help you plan your visit more effectively.

During the dry season, which typically spans from April to October, you can expect warm and pleasant weather with average temperatures ranging from 75°F to 85°F (24°C to 29°C). The skies are generally clear, and rain showers are infrequent, making it an ideal time for outdoor activities and exploring Kauai's breathtaking beaches and trails.

On the other hand, the wet season, from November to March, brings higher chances of rain and slightly cooler temperatures ranging from 70°F to 80°F (21°C to 27°C). The island's lush greenery thrives during this time, creating stunning landscapes and waterfalls. Despite the rain, Kauai's charm remains undeniable, and you can still enjoy plenty of indoor attractions and activities during occasional showers.

Peak Season vs. Off-Season Travel

Kauai experiences peak tourist traffic during the dry season, especially from mid-December to mid-April when travelers flock to escape the cold weather in other parts of the world. The island's popularity during this time means higher accommodation rates and increased crowds at popular tourist spots.

For a more tranquil and budget-friendly experience, consider visiting during the off-season, from mid-April to mid-December. The weather remains inviting, and you can take advantage of lower hotel rates and fewer tourists. Keep in mind that some attractions and tour operators may have reduced schedules during the off-season, so it's essential to plan your activities accordingly.

Special Events and Festivals

Kauai celebrates its vibrant culture and traditions through a variety of special events and festivals throughout the year.

Some of the notable ones include

1. Waimea Town Celebration (February): This week-long festival showcases Hawaiian culture, with events such as hula performances, traditional games, and a lively parade.

2. Prince Kuhio Day (March): Honoring Prince Jonah Kuhio Kalaniana'ole, a beloved figure in Hawaiian history, this day features ceremonies, music, and cultural demonstrations.

3. Kauai Polynesian Festival (May): Immerse yourself in the dances, music, and artistry of Polynesia during this vibrant cultural festival.

4. Koloa Plantation Days (July): Celebrating Kauai's sugar plantation heritage, this ten-day festival includes live music, historical displays, and a rodeo.

5. Eo E Emalani I Alakai Festival (October): Commemorating Queen Emma's journey to the Alaka'i Swamp, this event includes a reenactment of her procession and cultural activities.

Climate-Specific Activities

Both the dry and wet seasons offer unique opportunities for activities on Kauai:

1. Dry Season Activities: Enjoy snorkeling, scuba diving, and surfing in the clear waters off Kauai's coastline. Hike along the Na Pali Coast for breathtaking views, and explore the Waimea Canyon, also known as the "Grand Canyon of the Pacific." Visit the Allerton Garden and McBryde Garden for an enchanting botanical experience.

2. Wet Season Activities: Witness the island's lush beauty at its peak by visiting waterfalls, such as Wailua Falls and Opaeka'a Falls, which flow more vigorously during this time. Take a boat tour along the Wailua River to experience the serenity of the island's waterways. Engage in indoor activities, such as visiting museums and attending cultural performances.

Detailed Breakdown of the Wet and Dry Seasons

Dry Season (April to October)

  - Average Temperatures: 75°F to 85°F (24°C to 29°C)

  - Rainfall: Low, occasional brief showers

  - Activities: Ideal for beach days, hiking, water sports, and exploring outdoor attractions

Wet Season (November to March)

  - Average Temperatures: 70°F to 80°F (21°C to 27°C)

  - Rainfall: Higher, with intermittent heavy showers

  - Activities: Enjoy lush landscapes, and indoor attractions, while witnessing dynamic waterfalls

Kauai offers a diverse range of experiences throughout the year, and the best time to visit largely depends on your preferences and interests. Whether you prefer the dry season's sunny skies or the wet season's lush greenery, Kauai's charm will captivate you no matter when you choose to visit.

Keep in mind the climate-specific activities and the array of festivals and events to make the most of your journey to the Garden Isle. Plan ahead, and prepare to be enchanted by the beauty and culture that Kauai has to offer.

Chapter Eleven

Unique Experiences in Kauai

Kauai, also known as the Garden Isle, offers an array of unique experiences that go beyond typical tourist attractions. In this chapter, we will delve into the lesser-known activities and adventures off the beaten path, as well as the immersive cultural experiences that allow you to connect with the heart and soul of the island. Whether you are an adrenaline junkie seeking thrilling adventures or a cultural enthusiast looking to embrace the traditions of Kauai's people, this chapter will open up a world of possibilities for you to explore.

Smith's Tropical Paradise Luau: A Cultural Feast of Flavor and Entertainment

For guests wanting a true flavor of Hawaiian culture and a great evening of entertainment, Smith's Tropical Paradise Luau is a must-visit destination on Kauai. This immersive event delivers much more than a simple dinner—it's a voyage into the heart of Hawaiian customs, delivered against the backdrop of Kauai's beautiful natural splendor.

Cultural Immersion

At Smith's Tropical Paradise Luau, guests get the chance to dig deep into the traditions and customs of Hawaii. The luau opens with a heartfelt aloha welcome, setting the tone for an evening packed with music, dancing, and tales that represent the island's rich tradition. Traditional performances, like hula dances and Polynesian fire dancing, transport tourists to a bygone era, enabling them to connect with the essence of the islands.

The Feast

Central to the luau experience is the feast—aa tempting assortment of genuine Hawaiian foods that demonstrate the island's culinary diversity. From kalua pig, slow-cooked in an imu (subterranean oven), to fresh fish, tropical fruits, and poi (a traditional Hawaiian dish prepared from taro root), the menu is a celebration of local cuisine. The mix of tastes and fragrances produces an amazing eating experience that pays tribute to both the island's heritage and its present-day gourmet offerings.

Cost and Value

The cost of attending a luau at Smith's Tropical Paradise normally varies from $100 to $150 per adult, which includes entry to the feast and the colorful entertainment. While this could look like an investment, it's crucial to examine the entire value of the experience. Beyond the exquisite cuisine, the luau gives a true peek into Hawaiian culture that is frequently difficult to discover elsewhere. It's a chance to acquire insight into the tales, music, and dance that have defined the island's identity.

Safety Considerations

Luau locations, like Smith's Tropical Paradise, stress the safety and well-being of their visitors. Generally, luau gatherings are considered safe venues for people to enjoy the festivities. However, like with any event, it's recommended to be aware of your surroundings and comply with any safety precautions supplied by the hosts. Pay attention to announcements and take note of any safety advice offered throughout the luau.

Creating lasting memories

A visit to Smith's Tropical Paradise Luau is more than simply a dinner; it's a chance to make lasting memories and friendships. As you experience the delicacies of Hawaii, surrounded by the island's natural beauty and the rhythmic rhythms of traditional music, you'll find yourself carried away in the enchantment of the moment. It's an opportunity to not only enjoy a feast for the senses but to also get a greater grasp of Kauai's diverse cultural tapestry.

So, if you're looking for an evening of cultural immersion, gastronomic pleasures, and energetic entertainment, don't miss out on the opportunity to join Smith's Tropical Paradise Luau. Whether you're a solitary traveler, a couple on a romantic holiday, or a family wanting to enjoy a unique experience, the luau guarantees an exquisite evening that celebrates the heart and spirit of Kauai.

Wailua River Kayak and Secret Falls

Paddle up the scenic Wailua River, the only navigable river in Hawaii, to reach the hidden gem known as Secret Falls or

Uluwehi Falls. This tranquil journey takes you through lush rainforests and ancient Hawaiian sites, providing a glimpse into the island's rich history and natural beauty. Once at the falls, take a refreshing dip in the pool beneath the cascades and soak in the serenity of this remote oasis.

Kauai Backcountry Tubing Adventure

Embark on an exciting tubing adventure through the former irrigation canals of Kauai's sugar plantations. Float down the gentle currents, passing through tunnels and flumes that were once used to transport water to the fields. This unique experience offers a blend of history, adventure, and fun as you marvel at the engineering marvels of the past while enjoying the island's lush scenery.

ATV Off-Road Adventure: Unleash Your Inner Adventurer

For those wanting an adrenaline rush and an immersing experience in Kauai's natural surroundings, an ATV off-road adventure guarantees an amazing ride. Step away from the typical tourist paths and go deep into the island's rocky landscape for an experience that will leave you breathless in more ways than one.

The Thrill of Exploration

The heart-pounding adventure starts when you seize the reigns of an all-terrain vehicle, ready to tackle Kauai's untamed countryside. The red dirt lanes and rough terrain offer the ideal playground for off-road aficionados, and every twist and turn promises a burst of exhilaration.

Traverse Hidden Paths

As you journey through lush woods and meandering pathways, you'll find hidden passages that lead to Kauai's most well-kept secrets. Your skilled guides, well-versed in the island's geography, will bring you through terrain that's as demanding as it is enthralling. Traverse through lush forest and ascend height changes, all while experiencing the natural beauty of Kauai emerge before your eyes.

A Different Perspective

One of the delights of the ATV off-road experience is the ability to view the island's beauty from a unique perspective. While Kauai's well-known landmarks are undeniably magnificent, the off-road adventure brings you to perspectives that are distant from the traditional tourist destinations. You'll get a greater appreciation for the island's different landscapes as you stop to take in panoramic panoramas that are off the main route.

Immersive Natural Beauty

The excursion doesn't simply concentrate on the excitement; it's also a celebration of Kauai's unspoilt natural beauty. From the spectacular cliffs to the tranquil valleys, every minute on the ATV ride is a reminder of the island's raw and awe-inspiring scenery. Be prepared to meet creeks, traverse tiny bridges, and feel the genuine spirit of Kauai's wild side.

A Guided Journey

Safety and authenticity are important throughout the ATV off-road journey. Expert guides are available not just to walk you through the trails but also to give their views about the island's ecology, geology, and history. Their depth of expertise converts the trip into an educational excursion, expanding your comprehension of Kauai's natural treasures.

Creating lasting memories

An ATV off-road excursion isn't only a physical one; it's an emotional one as well. The rush of adrenaline, the awe-inspiring panoramas, and the feeling of success combine to produce memories that will remain with you long after your journey ends. It's an experience that gets you closer to the island, its scenery, and its people.

For those who desire an immersive journey that goes beyond the surface, the ATV off-road adventure in Kauai is a definite must. Get ready to experience the wind in your hair, the excitement in your heart, and the spirit of discovery in your soul as you travel terrains that are as wild and untamed as the Garden Isle itself. Experience Kauai from a fresh viewpoint, and let the ATV off-road experience be the highlight of your Hawaiian vacation.

Stargazing at the Summit of Mount Wai'ale'ale

Kauai is home to Mount Wai'ale'ale, one of the wettest places on Earth, and its summit offers an exceptional stargazing experience. Join a guided tour that takes you to the top of the mountain, where you can witness a stunning celestial display away from city lights. Marvel at the constellations, planets, and Milky Way, while learning about the cultural significance of the night sky in Hawaiian traditions.

Immersive Cultural Experiences

Hawaiian Luaus

Immerse yourself in the spirit of aloha by attending a traditional Hawaiian luau. These festive gatherings showcase the island's rich cultural heritage through music, dance, and delectable island cuisine. Witness captivating hula performances, listen to the melodious tunes of ukuleles, and savor the flavors of kalua pork, poi, and other Hawaiian delicacies.

Hawaiian Cultural Workshops

Participate in cultural workshops that offer hands-on experiences in various Hawaiian arts and crafts. Learn the art of lei-making using fresh flowers and foliage, try your hand at traditional hula or ukulele lessons, and discover the ancient Hawaiian practices of lauhala weaving or tapa cloth making. These workshops provide a deeper understanding of the island's cultural legacy and provide you with a unique keepsake to cherish.

Visiting Heiau (Hawaiian Temples)

Kauai is home to several ancient heiau, sacred Hawaiian temples that were once central to religious and cultural practices. Visiting these historical sites offers a chance to connect with the spiritual essence of the island. Remember to be respectful and follow cultural protocols when exploring these sacred grounds.

Kapa Making and Dyeing

Delve into the art of kapa making, a traditional Hawaiian fabric made from the inner bark of the wauke (paper mulberry) tree. Join a kapa-making workshop to learn about the intricate process of creating these beautiful textiles. Additionally, explore natural dyeing techniques, where you can use plants and minerals to add vibrant colors to your kapa creations.

Hawaiian Blessing and Ceremony

Receiving a Hawaiian blessing or participating in a sacred ceremony is a heartwarming tradition. These rituals are performed by kupuna (elders) or cultural practitioners and seek to bring harmony, protection, and positive energy into your life.

Whether you're starting a new chapter or simply seeking a deeper connection with the island, a Hawaiian blessing can be a profound and moving experience.

Kauai's unique experiences are not only thrilling but also enriching, providing travelers with a deeper understanding of the island's heritage and natural wonders. From exploring the hidden gems of the Nā Pali Coast to immersing yourself in Hawaiian cultural workshops, Kauai promises an unforgettable journey filled with adventure, discovery, and heartfelt connections. Embrace the spirit of aloha and let the Garden Isle leave a lasting imprint on your soul.

Chapter Twelve

Recommended Itineraries

When visiting Kauai, it's essential to plan your itinerary to make the most of your time on the Garden Isle. Whether you have a short 3-day stay or a more leisurely 7-day trip, we have carefully crafted two recommended itineraries to cater to different preferences and interests. These itineraries will help you explore the best of Kauai's natural wonders, cultural heritage, and adventurous activities.

Three-Day Itinerary for First-Time Visitors

Day 1: Exploring Kauai's North Shore

- Start your day with a hearty breakfast at a local cafe in Hanalei town. Try the Hawaiian favorite "Loco Moco" or indulge in fresh tropical fruits and pastries.

- Head to Hanalei Bay, a picturesque crescent-shaped beach perfect for swimming and sunbathing. Consider taking a surf lesson or renting a stand-up paddleboard to experience the waves.

- For a dose of history and culture, visit the Waioli Mission House and Church, a well-preserved historic site that provides insight into Kauai's missionary past.

- Enjoy a leisurely lunch in Hanalei and savor some delicious poke bowls or food truck specialties.

- In the afternoon, take a scenic drive along the North Shore, stopping at viewpoints like Kilauea Lighthouse and the Hanalei Valley Lookout.

- Conclude your day with a relaxing sunset beach walk at Anini Beach or Ke'e Beach, soaking in the natural beauty of the island.

Day 2: Waimea Canyon and West Side Adventures

- Rise early to make the most of your day exploring Waimea Canyon, often referred to as the "Grand Canyon of the Pacific." Take the Waimea Canyon Drive and make several stops at designated viewpoints to admire the stunning vistas.

- Continue your journey to Koke'e State Park, where you can embark on various hiking trails through lush forests and unique landscapes. The Awaawapuhi Trail and the Canyon Trail are highly recommended for their breathtaking panoramas.

- Have a picnic lunch amid nature's beauty in Koke'e State Park.

- After lunch, head to the West Side of Kauai and visit the historic Russian Fort Elizabeth State Historical Park, which offers glimpses of Hawaii's past with its well-preserved fortification.

- Relax at Polihale State Park, known for its long stretch of sandy beach and unmatched sunsets. Please note that the road to Polihale can be rough, so a 4WD vehicle is recommended.

- Wrap up your day with a sumptuous dinner at one of the local restaurants in Waimea town.

Day 3: East Side and Wailua River Adventures

- Begin your day with a sunrise visit to Opaekaa Falls, an easily accessible and captivating waterfall on the East Side of the island.

- Embark on a Wailua River tour to witness the enchanting Fern Grotto and the sacred Wailua River Valley. Options include kayak tours, riverboat cruises, or guided stand-up paddleboarding.

- Take a short hike to the Opaeka'a Falls Lookout for a panoramic view of the river valley.

- Treat yourself to a delightful lunch in Kapaa town, known for its vibrant food scene and local eateries.

- Spend the afternoon relaxing at one of Kauai's beautiful beaches, such as Lydgate Beach Park, known for its protected swimming area and snorkeling opportunities.

- As the sun sets on your final day, reflect on your Kauai adventure while dining at a seaside restaurant in Kapaa or Lihue.

7-Day Itinerary for Exploring Kauai Thoroughly

Day 1: Arrival and South Shore Exploration

- Arrive on Kauai and settle into your accommodation on the South Shore, either in Poipu or Koloa.

- Begin your exploration with a visit to Poipu Beach Park, one of the most popular beaches on the island, ideal for swimming, snorkeling, and sunbathing.

- Enjoy lunch at one of the nearby beachside restaurants or explore local food trucks for a taste of Kauai's diverse cuisine.

- Visit the Spouting Horn, a natural wonder where seawater shoots up through lava tubes, creating a mesmerizing display.

- In the afternoon, consider exploring the nearby Allerton Garden or McBryde Garden for a unique botanical experience.

- Unwind and enjoy the sunset at Shipwreck Beach or Brennecke's Beach.

Day 2: Napali Coast Boat Tour

- Embark on an early morning boat tour of the iconic Napali Coast. Witness breathtaking sea cliffs, sea caves, and cascading waterfalls. Some tours offer snorkeling opportunities and a chance to encounter marine life like dolphins and turtles.

- These boat tours can be quite exhilarating, so take motion sickness precautions if needed.

- After returning from the boat tour, relax at your accommodation or opt for a rejuvenating spa experience.

Day 3: Exploring Kauai's North Shore

- You can repeat the 3-Day Itinerary for First-Time Visitors, focusing on Hanalei town and the stunning North Shore attractions.

Day 4: Discovering the East Side and Wailua River

- Follow the 3-Day Itinerary for First-Time Visitors, focusing on the East Side and the scenic Wailua River.

Day 5: Adventure in the Garden Isle's Heartland

- Begin your day with a trip to the lush and serene Wailua Falls, a popular waterfall with scenic overlooks.

- Continue to explore the interior of Kauai by visiting the quaint town of Kapaa and exploring its unique boutiques and art galleries.

- Have lunch at one of the local eateries and try some fresh, farm-to-table dishes.

- In the afternoon, embark on an ATV tour or a zipline adventure to immerse yourself in Kauai's adventurous side.

- Consider ending your day with a relaxing sunset beach stroll on Kealia Beach.

Day 6: Waimea Canyon and Kauai's West Side

- Follow the 3-Day Itinerary for First-Time Visitors, focusing on Waimea Canyon and the West Side.

Day 7: Last Day Explorations

- On your final day, choose your favorite spots from the previous days to revisit or explore areas you haven't had the chance to see yet.

- Spend your last moments on the island cherishing the natural beauty and unique experiences of Kauai.

Essential Items for Your Travel Kit

Before embarking on your Kauai adventure, it's crucial to pack a well-prepared travel kit to ensure a safe and enjoyable trip. Here are some essential items you should consider bringing:

- Sun Protection: Sunscreen with a high SPF, sunglasses, and a wide-brimmed hat to shield yourself from the intense Hawaiian sun.

- Insect Repellent: Keep those pesky bugs away with an effective insect repellent to avoid discomfort during outdoor activities.

- Rain Gear: A lightweight, waterproof jacket or poncho can come in handy, as Kauai's weather can be unpredictable.

- Hiking Gear: If you plan to explore Kauai's trails, comfortable hiking shoes or sandals are a must, along with a daypack to carry water, snacks, and a first aid kit.

- Swim Gear: Don't forget your swimsuit, beach towels, and beach essentials like a beach mat or chair, snorkeling gear (if you have your own), and water shoes for rocky shorelines.

- Water Bottle: Stay hydrated throughout your adventures by carrying a reusable water bottle. Kauai's tropical climate demands frequent hydration, especially during outdoor activities.

- Camera and Binoculars: Capture the breathtaking landscapes and wildlife encounters with a good-quality camera. Binoculars are also handy for spotting distant waterfalls, marine life, and birds.

- Portable Phone Charger: Ensure your phone stays charged for GPS navigation, taking photos, and staying connected. A portable charger will be a lifesaver, especially during long excursions.

- Travel Documents: Keep your passport, visa, driver's licence, and any necessary travel permits in a secure, waterproof bag. Also, store electronic copies in your email or cloud storage as a backup.

- Cash and Credit Cards: While credit cards are widely accepted, some smaller establishments may prefer cash. Have a mix of both, and inform your bank of your travel dates to avoid card issues.

- Medications and First Aid Kit: Bring any necessary prescription medications and a basic first aid kit containing bandages, antiseptic ointment, pain relievers, and motion sickness medication if needed.

- Toiletries: Pack travel-sized toiletries, including shampoo, conditioner, body wash, toothbrush, and toothpaste.

- Beach Bag: A spacious beach bag will come in handy for carrying your essentials to the beach and keeping sand-free.

- Travel Adapter and Power Strip: If you're visiting from another country, ensure you have the appropriate travel adapter to charge your devices. A power strip can be useful when there are limited electrical outlets in your accommodation.

- Guidebooks and Maps: While you can find a lot of information online, having a physical guidebook and a detailed map of Kauai can be valuable when exploring the island.

Remember that Kauai's natural beauty and adventurous spirit are best experienced with proper preparation and respect for the environment. Leave no trace and be mindful of the fragile ecosystems during your journey.

Kauai, the Garden Isle, offers an abundance of experiences for travelers seeking pristine landscapes, thrilling activities, and a taste of Hawaiian culture. The 3-day and 7-day itineraries provide an excellent overview of the island's highlights, but don't hesitate to customize your trip based on your interests and time constraints.

As you embark on your Kauai adventure, immerse yourself in the stunning vistas, embrace the aloha spirit of the locals, and create cherished memories that will last a lifetime. Whether you're exploring the lush Waimea Canyon, relaxing on beautiful beaches, or taking in the mesmerizing Napali Coast, Kauai's unique charm and natural wonders are sure to leave a lasting impression.

Mahalo for choosing Kauai as your destination. We hope this comprehensive travel guide has equipped you with the knowledge and inspiration to make the most of your journey. Enjoy your time in paradise and aloha until we meet again. Safe travels!

Chapter Thirteen

Health Tips for Travelers

Kauai, with its lush landscapes and inviting beaches, is a dream destination for many travelers. However, it's essential to prioritize your health and well-being while exploring this beautiful island. In this comprehensive chapter, we will delve into the necessary vaccinations and health precautions for traveling to Kauai, common health issues you might encounter, the availability of medical facilities and services on the island, and how to handle emergencies effectively. Moreover, we'll provide a list of important emergency numbers and services to keep you prepared for any unforeseen circumstances.

Necessary Vaccinations and Health Precautions

Before embarking on your journey to Kauai, it's crucial to be up-to-date with routine vaccinations recommended by your home country's health authorities. These may include vaccines for measles, mumps, rubella, diphtheria, tetanus, pertussis, polio, and influenza.

Additionally, travelers should consider the following vaccinations:

- Hepatitis A and B: Hepatitis A can be contracted through contaminated food and water, and Hepatitis B through blood or sexual contact. Both vaccines are essential, especially if you plan to try local cuisine or engage in adventurous activities.

- Typhoid: Caused by consuming contaminated food or water, a typhoid vaccine is advisable for travelers who may be exposed to local dining options.

- Rabies: Although the risk of rabies transmission from animals on Kauai is low, it's recommended for travelers who will be participating in outdoor activities or working closely with animals.

- Japanese Encephalitis: While Kauai itself doesn't have a high risk of Japanese encephalitis, if you're planning to visit other parts of Hawaii or nearby countries where the disease is prevalent, consider getting vaccinated.

- Meningococcal: This vaccine is recommended for travelers engaging in close contact with locals or participating in large gatherings or events.

Remember to consult with a travel health specialist or your healthcare provider at least 4-6 weeks before your trip to ensure you receive the necessary vaccinations and health advice tailored to your individual needs.

In addition to vaccinations, follow these health precautions during your stay on Kauai:

- Stay Hydrated: The tropical climate of Kauai can be hot and humid, so it's essential to drink plenty of water to avoid dehydration.

- Protect Yourself from the Sun: Use sunscreen with a high SPF, wear wide-brimmed hats, and wear lightweight, breathable clothing to shield yourself from the sun's strong rays.

- Insect Protection: Use insect repellent with DEET to prevent mosquito bites, especially during dusk and dawn when mosquitoes are most active.

- Food and Water Safety: Consume food from reputable establishments and drink bottled water to avoid potential foodborne illnesses.

- Ocean Safety: Be cautious when swimming in the ocean and pay attention to local safety advisories. Strong currents and high surf can be dangerous, even for experienced swimmers.

Dealing with Common Health Issues

Despite taking necessary precautions, travelers may encounter common health issues during their visit to Kauai.

- Sunburn: If you get sunburned, seek shade immediately and apply aloe vera gel or moisturizing lotion to soothe the affected area. Stay hydrated and avoid further sun exposure until the burn heals.

- Heat Exhaustion and Heatstroke: Symptoms include heavy sweating, weakness, nausea, and confusion. Move to a cooler place, rest, and drink cool water. If symptoms persist or worsen, seek medical attention.

- Traveler's Diarrhea: This can be caused by consuming contaminated food or water. Stay hydrated and consider over-the-counter medications to manage symptoms. If diarrhea is severe or persists, consult a doctor.

- Insect Bites and Stings: Clean the affected area with soap and water, and apply antihistamine cream or calamine lotion to reduce itching and inflammation.

Medical Facilities and Services on the Island

Kauai has several medical facilities to cater to the health needs of both residents and travelers. The main hospital on the island is Wilcox Medical Center, located in Lihue. It offers a range of medical services, including emergency care, inpatient treatment, and outpatient clinics. Additionally, there are urgent care centers and private medical practices scattered across the island.

For minor health issues, you can visit local pharmacies, which offer over-the-counter medications and advice from pharmacists. Be sure to carry your health insurance information and contact your insurance provider before seeking medical care to understand your coverage options.

How to Handle Emergencies While on Kauai

In the event of a medical emergency on Kauai, call 911 or 1911 for immediate assistance. The emergency responders will dispatch appropriate services, including ambulance transportation if necessary. Be prepared to provide your location, the nature of the emergency, and any relevant medical information.

If you're not facing a life-threatening emergency but still require medical attention, you can visit the nearest urgent care center or contact your medical provider for guidance.

Knowing Emergency Numbers and Services

Keep a list of important emergency numbers handy while traveling on Kauai

- Emergency Services (Police/Fire/Ambulance): Dial ☎ 911

- Kauai Police Department Non-Emergency: ☎ (808) 241-1711

- Kauai Fire Department Non-Emergency: ☎ (808) 241-4980

- Poison Control Center: 1-800-222-1222

Prioritizing your health and well-being while traveling to Kauai is of utmost importance. By being proactive and following health precautions, you can enjoy a safe and memorable trip on the Garden Isle. Ensure you have the necessary vaccinations, protect yourself from the elements, and be aware of common health issues that travelers might face.

Familiarize yourself with the medical facilities and services available on the island, and in case of an emergency, know the appropriate contact numbers. With proper preparation and care, you can fully immerse yourself in the beauty of Kauai and create lasting memories of your journey to this tropical paradise.

Bonus Chapter

30 Best Places to Visit and When

Kauai, known as the Garden Isle, is a treasure trove of natural beauty and captivating landscapes. This chapter highlights the top destinations on the island that every traveler should experience. Each place is unique and offers something different, from lush rainforests and cascading waterfalls to pristine beaches and dramatic cliffs. Additionally, we'll provide you with insights into the best timeframes to visit these locations, taking into account weather conditions, crowd levels, and seasonal attractions.

1. Na Pali Coast

The Na Pali Coast is an awe-inspiring stretch of coastline that boasts dramatic sea cliffs, lush valleys, and cascading waterfalls. Accessible by boat, helicopter, or hiking, this rugged paradise offers breathtaking views that will leave you in awe. The best time to visit the Na Pali Coast is during the dry season, which typically runs from April to October. During these months, the sea is calmer, making boat tours and snorkeling more enjoyable.

Hiking enthusiasts can explore the famous Kalalau Trail, but be sure to check the weather forecast and trail conditions before embarking on this challenging journey.

2. Waimea Canyon

Dubbed the "Grand Canyon of the Pacific," Waimea Canyon is a geological marvel that stretches approximately 14 miles long and over 3,600 feet deep. The vibrant hues of red, orange, and green create a stunning visual display. The best time to visit Waimea Canyon is during the drier months of May to September, when the skies are clearer, and offer the most picturesque vistas. Consider taking a guided tour or hiking along the trails for the best views and photo opportunities.

3. Wailua Falls

Wailua Falls is a breathtaking double-tiered waterfall located just a short drive from Lihue. This iconic waterfall was made famous by the television series "Fantasy Island." The best time to visit Wailua Falls is during the rainy season, typically from November to March, when the water flow is at its peak, creating a magnificent cascade. Be sure to exercise caution and follow safety guidelines while viewing the falls, as the rocks can be slippery.

4. Hanalei Bay

Hanalei Bay is a picturesque crescent-shaped bay on the North Shore of Kauai, surrounded by verdant mountains and swaying palm trees. This idyllic spot is perfect for water activities such as swimming, paddleboarding, and snorkeling. The best time to visit Hanalei Bay is during the summer months from June to September when the ocean conditions are calmer and more suitable for swimming. The bay's stunning sunsets make it an excellent location for a relaxing evening by the beach.

5. Poipu Beach

On the South Shore of Kauai lies Poipu Beach, a popular destination known for its golden sands and excellent snorkeling opportunities. This family-friendly beach is a great spot to spot Hawaiian green sea turtles and monk seals basking in the sun. The best time to visit Poipu Beach is during the dry season from April to October when the waters are clear and calm, making it ideal for snorkeling and swimming.

6. Kalalau Lookout

For panoramic views of the Napali Coast, make your way to the Kalalau Lookout in Koke'e State Park. This viewpoint offers a breathtaking vista of the coastline and the deep valleys below. The best time to visit the Kalalau Lookout is early in the morning when the skies are clear, providing better visibility and fewer clouds obstructing the view.

7. Spouting Horn

Spouting Horn is a natural wonder located on Kauai's South Shore near Poipu Beach. This blowhole shoots seawater high into the air, creating an impressive spectacle. The best time to visit Spouting Horn is during high tide, as the water pressure is stronger, resulting in more spectacular eruptions. Additionally, witnessing the sunset from this location adds a touch of magic to the experience.

8. Limahuli Garden and Preserve

If you're a nature enthusiast, a visit to the Limahuli Garden and Preserve on the North Shore is a must. This botanical garden showcases native Hawaiian plants and offers a glimpse into the island's rich ecological history.

The best time to visit the Limahuli Garden is in the early morning or late afternoon, when the weather is cooler, and the lighting enhances the beauty of the lush landscape.

9. Tunnels Beach

Tunnels Beach, also known as Makua Beach, is a renowned snorkeling and diving spot on the North Shore. The underwater lava tubes and coral formations make it a captivating underwater playground for marine life enthusiasts. The best time to visit Tunnels Beach is during the summer months, when the water is calmer and visibility is at its best for snorkeling and scuba diving.

10. Hanakapiai Falls

Hanakapiai Falls is a majestic 300-foot waterfall located in the heart of the Napali Coast via the challenging Kalalau Trail. This strenuous hike rewards adventurous travelers with a mesmerizing view of the waterfall amidst a lush tropical setting. The best time to hike to Hanakapiai Falls is during the dry season when the trail conditions are more favorable. Remember to obtain a hiking permit and be prepared with proper hiking gear.

11. Maha'ulepu Heritage Trail

The Maha'ulepu Heritage Trail is a beautiful coastal path that offers scenic views of the rugged coastline and the Pacific Ocean. This leisurely hike is perfect for nature lovers and history enthusiasts, as it passes ancient Hawaiian archaeological sites. The best time to walk the Maha'ulepu Heritage Trail is in the early morning or late afternoon, as the temperature is more pleasant, and the lighting is ideal for photography.

12. Kilauea Point National Wildlife Refuge

For birdwatching and panoramic views, visit the Kilauea Point National Wildlife Refuge on the North Shore. This protected area is home to a variety of seabirds, including the iconic red-footed boobies and Laysan albatrosses. The best time to visit the Kilauea Point National Wildlife Refuge is during the breeding season, from November to June when you have the opportunity to observe nesting seabirds and their adorable chicks.

13. Secret Beach (Kauapea Beach)

True to its name, Secret Beach is a secluded and uncrowded beach located on the North Shore of Kauai.

Its golden sands stretch for miles, making it an ideal spot for a relaxing day by the ocean. The best time to visit Secret Beach is during the drier months from May to September when the ocean conditions are safer for swimming and sunbathing.

14. Waimea Town

Explore the charming town of Waimea, known for its rich history and vibrant cultural heritage. Visit the Waimea Historical Museum to learn about the island's past and the significance of Captain Cook's landing. The best time to visit Waimea Town is during the annual Waimea Town Celebration, held in February, where you can experience the local traditions, live music, and delicious food.

15. Opaekaa Falls

Opaekaa Falls is a scenic waterfall located in Wailua River State Park, easily accessible by car. The falls cascade into a picturesque pool, surrounded by lush greenery. The best time to visit Opaekaa Falls is after heavy rainfall, when the waterfall is at its most impressive and the pool is filled with cascading water. Consider visiting during the morning hours when the lighting is ideal for capturing stunning photographs.

16. Allerton Garden and McBryde Garden

Located on the South Shore, Allerton Garden and McBryde Garden are part of the National Tropical Botanical Garden, offering an enchanting experience for plant enthusiasts and garden lovers alike. These lush gardens showcase an impressive collection of tropical plants, including rare and endangered species. The best time to visit Allerton Garden and McBryde Garden is during the dry season from April to October when the weather is more predictable, allowing for a pleasant stroll through the well-maintained paths.

17. Polihale State Park

For an off-the-beaten-path adventure, head to Polihale State Park, a remote and wild beach on the western side of Kauai. This expansive stretch of golden sand offers mesmerizing views of the Napali Coast and the opportunity to witness spectacular sunsets. The best time to visit Polihale State Park is during the dry season when the dirt road leading to the park is more accessible. Be prepared for a bumpy ride, as reaching the park requires a 4WD vehicle.

18. Makauwahi Cave Reserve

Explore the Makauwahi Cave Reserve, an archaeological and ecological treasure located near Maha'ulepu Beach. This unique limestone cave system offers a glimpse into Kauai's ancient history and the island's diverse flora and fauna. The best time to visit Makauwahi Cave Reserve is during low tide when guided tours are available, providing an informative and educational experience.

19. Kauai Coffee Company

Coffee enthusiasts should not miss a visit to the Kauai Coffee Company, the largest coffee plantation in Hawaii. Take a guided tour of the plantation to learn about the coffee-growing process and sample a variety of freshly brewed coffee. The best time to visit the Kauai Coffee Company is during the harvesting season, which typically runs from September to December when you can witness the coffee cherries being picked and processed.

20. Hanapepe Town

Embrace the artistic and laid-back vibes of Hanapepe Town, often referred to as Kauai's biggest little town. Stroll through the charming streets filled with art galleries, boutique shops, and local eateries. The best time to visit Hanapepe Town is during

Friday Night Art Walks when the town comes alive with live music, art displays, and food vendors, creating a lively and festive atmosphere.

21. Anahola Beach Park

Anahola Beach Park, located on the eastern coast, is a tranquil and family-friendly beach surrounded by a protective reef, making it ideal for swimming and picnicking. The best time to visit Anahola Beach Park is during the weekdays when the beach is less crowded, allowing for a more peaceful and relaxing experience.

22. Ke'e Beach

Nestled at the end of the road on the North Shore, Ke'e Beach is a serene and picturesque spot to relax and enjoy the stunning views of the Napali Coast. The best time to visit Ke'e Beach is during the summer months when the ocean is calmer, providing safer swimming conditions and better visibility for snorkeling.

23. Koke'e State Park

Immerse yourself in the natural beauty of Koke'e State Park, home to vast forests, unique plant species, and numerous hiking trails. The best time to visit Koke'e State Park is during the drier months of April to October when the trails are less muddy and the weather is more suitable for outdoor activities.

24. Nounou Mountain (Sleeping Giant) Trail

For panoramic views of Kauai's east side, embark on the Nounou Mountain Trail, also known as the Sleeping Giant. This moderate hike takes you to the summit of the mountain, rewarding hikers with breathtaking vistas of the coastline and surrounding landscapes. The best time to hike the Nounou Mountain Trail is in the early morning to avoid the midday heat and enjoy the sunrise views.

25. Smith's Tropical Paradise Luau

Experience the spirit of aloha at Smith's Tropical Paradise Luau, where you can indulge in traditional Hawaiian cuisine and enjoy captivating performances showcasing hula, music, and storytelling. The best time to attend Smith's Tropical Paradise Luau is during the evening to witness the enchanting torch-lighting ceremony and the mesmerizing Polynesian dance performances under the stars.

26. Haena Beach Park

Haena Beach Park is a tranquil and scenic spot on the North Shore, perfect for picnicking, beachcombing, and relaxing. The best time to visit Haena Beach Park is during the summer months, as the ocean conditions are generally calmer, creating a safer environment for swimming and enjoying the shoreline.

27. Kauai Museum

Learn about the island's history and cultural heritage at the Kauai Museum in Lihue. The museum's exhibits feature heirlooms, artworks, and historical displays, providing insight into Kauai's past. The best time to visit the Kauai Museum is during the weekdays when the museum is less crowded, allowing for a more intimate and immersive experience.

28. Pali Ke Kua Beach (Hideaways Beach)

Pali Ke Kua Beach, also known as Hideaways Beach, is a hidden gem located near Princeville. Accessible via a short hike, this secluded beach offers a sense of privacy and seclusion, making it an excellent spot for sunbathing and relaxation.

The best time to visit Pali Ke Kua Beach is during the summer months when the ocean conditions are calmer and the beach is less affected by winter swells.

29. Hanalei Valley Lookout

For a breathtaking view of Hanalei Valley and the taro fields below, make your way to the Hanalei Valley Lookout on the North Shore. The best time to visit the Hanalei Valley Lookout is in the morning or late afternoon, when the lighting accentuates the beauty of the valley and the surrounding mountains.

30. Fern Grotto

Take a boat tour to the iconic Fern Grotto, a natural amphitheater covered in lush ferns and tropical foliage. This enchanting spot is a popular wedding destination due to its natural beauty and serene ambiance. The best time to visit the Fern Grotto is during the drier months of May to September, as heavy rain can sometimes make access to the grotto challenging.

Kauai's top destinations offer an unparalleled array of natural wonders and cultural experiences that will leave you mesmerized and inspired.

Whether you are an adventure seeker, a nature lover, or a cultural enthusiast, each place on this comprehensive list has its unique charm and allure.

Remember to plan your visit according to the recommended timeframes to make the most of your experience and ensure an unforgettable journey through the Garden Isle. From the stunning cliffs of the Na Pali Coast to the tranquil shores of Hanalei Bay, Kauai's beauty is bound to capture your heart and create memories that will last a lifetime. So, pack your bags, embark on your Kauai adventure, and immerse yourself in the magic of this island paradise. Aloha and safe travels!

Recommended Timeframes for Visiting Each Place

1. Na Pali Coast: The best time to visit the Na Pali Coast is during the dry season, which typically runs from April to October. During these months, the weather is generally more stable, and there is less chance of rain, making boat tours and hiking the Kalalau Trail more enjoyable.

The sea is calmer, providing better conditions for snorkeling and exploring the coastline. However, do keep in mind that the summer months can be busier with tourists, so consider visiting in the shoulder months of April, May, September, or October for a more serene experience.

2. Waimea Canyon: The best time to visit Waimea Canyon is during the drier months of May to September. During this period, the skies are clearer, offering the most picturesque vistas of the canyon's vibrant colors. The winter months (November to March) can bring more rain, leading to cloud cover obstructing the views. To fully enjoy the beauty of Waimea Canyon, aim for a visit during the dry season.

3. Wailua Falls: The best time to visit Wailua Falls is during the rainy season, typically from November to March. During this time, the waterfall's water flow is at its peak, creating a magnificent cascade. However, keep in mind that the trails leading to the falls might be muddier during this season, so wear appropriate footwear and exercise caution while exploring the area.

4. Hanalei Bay: The best time to visit Hanalei Bay is during the summer months from June to September. During this time, the

ocean conditions are calmer, making it ideal for swimming, paddleboarding, and snorkeling. The bay's stunning sunsets are an added bonus during the summer evenings.

5. Poipu Beach: The best time to visit Poipu Beach is during the dry season from April to October. During these months, the waters are clearer and calmer, providing excellent conditions for snorkeling and swimming. However, keep an eye out for seasonal visitors like Hawaiian monk seals, as they may rest on the shore during certain times of the year.

6. Kalalau Lookout: The best time to visit the Kalalau Lookout is early in the morning when the skies are clear, providing better visibility of the Napali Coast. Cloud cover tends to increase throughout the day, which can obstruct the stunning views. Plan to arrive at the lookout during sunrise for a breathtaking sight.

7. Spouting Horn: The best time to visit Spouting Horn is during high tide when the water pressure is stronger, resulting in more spectacular eruptions. For the best experience, check the local tide schedule and plan your visit accordingly.

8. Limahuli Garden and Preserve: The best time to visit Limahuli Garden is during the early morning or late afternoon

when the weather is cooler, and the lighting enhances the beauty of the garden's lush landscape. Aim for weekdays to avoid larger crowds and enjoy a more serene experience.

9. Tunnels Beach: The best time to visit Tunnels Beach is during the summer months when the water is calmer and visibility is at its best for snorkeling and scuba diving. Keep an eye on weather conditions and ocean advisories to ensure safe water activities.

10. Hanakapiai Falls: The best time to hike to Hanakapiai Falls is during the dry season when the trail conditions are more favorable. The muddy and slippery conditions of the trail are less of a concern during the drier months, making it a safer and more enjoyable trek.

11. Maha'ulepu Heritage Trail: The best time to walk the Maha'ulepu Heritage Trail is during the early morning or late afternoon. The temperature is more pleasant during these times, and the lighting is ideal for photography, accentuating the beauty of the coastal views.

12. Kilauea Point National Wildlife Refuge: The best time to visit the Kilauea Point National Wildlife Refuge is during the breeding season from November to June. During this time, you

have the opportunity to observe nesting seabirds, including the iconic red-footed boobies and Laysan albatrosses.

13. Secret Beach (Kauapea Beach): The best time to visit Secret Beach is during the drier months from May to September when the ocean conditions are safer for swimming and sunbathing. However, be cautious of strong currents and potential high surf during the winter months.

14. Waimea Town: The best time to visit Waimea Town is during the annual Waimea Town Celebration, held in February. This lively festival allows you to experience the local traditions, live music, and delicious food, providing a deeper connection to the island's culture.

15. Anahola Beach Park: The best time to visit Anahola Beach Park is during the weekdays when the beach is less crowded, allowing for a more peaceful and relaxing experience. Consider packing a picnic and enjoying the tranquility of this scenic spot.

16. Ke'e Beach: The best time to visit Ke'e Beach is during the summer months when the ocean conditions are calmer, providing safer swimming conditions and better visibility for

snorkeling. However, always be mindful of any ocean advisories or warnings.

17. Koke'e State Park: The best time to visit Koke'e State Park is during the drier months of April to October. The trails are less muddy during this time, and the weather is more suitable for outdoor activities, such as hiking and exploring the unique plant life.

18. Nounou Mountain (Sleeping Giant) Trail: The best time to hike the Nounou Mountain Trail is during the early morning to avoid the midday heat and enjoy the sunrise views. Be sure to wear proper hiking gear and bring plenty of water for this moderate hike.

19. Pali Ke Kua Beach (Hideaways Beach): The best time to visit Pali Ke Kua Beach is during the summer months when the ocean conditions are calmer, making it safer for swimming and sunbathing. The beach's secluded location offers a sense of privacy, allowing for a relaxing beach experience.

While Kauai's beauty is enchanting year-round, planning your visit according to these recommended timeframes will enhance your experience and allow you to make the most of each destination's unique offerings. Always be mindful of weather conditions and any advisories to ensure a safe and enjoyable exploration of the Garden Isle.

Chapter Fourteen

Reasons to Visit Kauai

Embrace the Enchanting Beauty and Charm

Kauai, often referred to as the Garden Isle, is a mesmerizing destination that captivates the hearts of travelers from around the world. Nestled within the Hawaiian archipelago, this lush paradise boasts a plethora of unique selling points that set it apart from other destinations. From its breathtaking natural wonders to its vibrant cultural offerings, Kauai has something to offer every traveler seeking a once-in-a-lifetime experience. In this chapter, we delve deep into the reasons why you should choose Kauai as your next travel destination.

Pristine Natural Landscapes

Kauai is renowned for its pristine and untouched natural landscapes. The island's rugged coastline, lush rainforests, majestic waterfalls, and golden sand beaches create a picturesque scene that seems straight out of a postcard. Witness the awe-inspiring beauty of Waimea Canyon, often called the "Grand Canyon of the Pacific," and explore the dramatic cliffs of the Na Pali Coast, accessible by hiking, boat tours, or helicopter rides.

The Spirit of Aloha

Embrace the genuine and warm hospitality of the locals, who embody the spirit of aloha. Kauai's residents welcome visitors with open arms, making you feel like a part of their 'ohana (family). Immerse yourself in the island's friendly atmosphere and embrace the aloha culture, which emphasizes love, respect, and unity.

Outdoor Adventure

For adventure seekers, Kauai is a playground of opportunities. Hike along challenging trails, such as the Kalalau Trail, which leads you to secluded beaches and breathtaking vistas. Embark on thrilling ziplining adventures, kayak down scenic rivers, or take a stand-up paddleboarding journey along the calm waters of Hanalei Bay.

Magnificent Waterfalls

Kauai is home to an array of stunning waterfalls that cascade down verdant cliffs. The iconic Wailua Falls, featured in the television show "Fantasy Island," is easily accessible and a must-see attraction. Additionally, the secluded Manawaiopuna Falls, often referred to as Jurassic Falls, can be viewed from helicopter tours for a truly unforgettable experience.

Pristine Beaches

Kauai offers a diverse range of beaches to suit every preference. Relax on the serene shores of Poipu Beach, renowned for its calm waters and ideal snorkeling conditions. Venture to the remote Polihale State Park for a secluded beach experience or admire the striking red sands of Kaihalulu Beach, also known as Red Sand Beach.

Cultural Experiences

Dive into Kauai's rich Hawaiian culture and heritage through various cultural experiences. Attend a traditional luau to savor authentic Hawaiian cuisine and witness hula performances that recount the island's history. Visit local museums and cultural centers to learn about the island's indigenous roots and traditions.

Film Locations

- Kauai's enchanting landscapes have served as the backdrop for numerous Hollywood films and TV shows. Movie buffs will recognize iconic locations from movies like "Jurassic Park," "Avatar," and "Indiana Jones and the Raiders of the Lost Ark." Take guided tours to explore these famous film sites and relive your favorite cinematic moments.

Unique Flora and Fauna

As the oldest island in the Hawaiian chain, Kauai boasts a diverse range of flora and fauna found nowhere else on Earth. Discover rare native plant and bird species in the Alaka'i Wilderness Preserve, a pristine and remote rainforest. Birdwatching enthusiasts will be thrilled to spot endangered native birds like the 'I'iwi and the Nene (Hawaiian goose).

Serene Sunrises and Sunsets

Greet the day with awe-inspiring sunrises over the Pacific Ocean. Head to the eastern shores of the island, such as Anahola Beach Park or Kealia Beach, to witness the sun's first rays illuminating the sky. At day's end, savor the stunning sunsets along the west coast, particularly from the cliffs of Polihale State Park or the Hanalei Pier.

Spiritual and Healing Energy

Many visitors to Kauai attest to feeling a special spiritual and healing energy on the island. Whether it's the serene atmosphere of Wailua Falls or the tranquility of Limahuli Garden and Preserve, Kauai's natural surroundings have a calming effect that encourages relaxation and introspection.

Whale Watching

From December to April, Kauai's waters become the stage for majestic humpback whales on their annual migration. Join a whale-watching tour to witness these gentle giants breaching and tail-slapping as they frolic in the Pacific Ocean, an experience that leaves a lasting impression.

Adventure Capital of Hawaii

Kauai's reputation as the adventure capital of Hawaii is well-deserved. Whether you're a seasoned adrenaline junkie or a novice seeking new thrills, Kauai has a diverse range of activities to suit every adventure level, from thrilling helicopter tours to heart-pounding ATV excursions.

Island Hopping Opportunities: Exploring Beyond Kauai

One of the most exciting elements of visiting Kauai is its strategic placement within the Hawaiian archipelago, which allows vacationers a unique opportunity for island hopping. While Kauai itself is a treasure trove of natural beauties and cultural experiences, it also offers a great starting point for exploring the other islands. Embarking on day excursions to Oahu, Maui, or the Big Island from Kauai enables you to enjoy the different beauty and attractions that each island has to offer.

Oahu: A Blend of Modernity and Tradition

Just a short flight away from Kauai, Oahu is a bustling island that elegantly integrates contemporary city life with Hawaiian customs. Upon arrival, the busy metropolis of Honolulu greets you with its vibrant atmosphere and prominent buildings. Visit Pearl Harbor to pay your respects and learn about a critical time in history. Delve into the heart of Polynesian culture at the Polynesian Cultural Center, where you can enjoy traditional dances, crafts, and food.

For visitors hoping to catch some waves, Waikiki Beach is famed for its surf-friendly waters and vibrant beach atmosphere.

Maui: The Land of Beauty and Adventure

Known as the Valley Isle, Maui is attractive with its various scenery and outdoor experiences. The sunrise from the top of Haleakala is a bucket-list moment, as the colors of dawn paint the sky above the beautiful crater. Hana Road provides a lovely journey through lush woods, waterfalls, and quiet ponds. Snorkeling fans can find heaven at Molokini Crater, a flourishing marine refuge. Don't forget to sample the native flavors of Maui, as the island has some of Hawaii's best farm-to-table food.

Big Island: A World of Contrasts

For an investigation of opposites, focus your eyes on the Big Island. The island's diversified terrain varies from the snow-capped summit of Mauna Kea to the streaming lava of Kilauea. Hawaii Volcanoes National Park shows the dramatic geological processes that have created the islands over millions of years. Immerse yourself in the island's traditional culture by visiting the Puuhonua o Honaunau National Historical Park, a holy location of refuge and healing. From lush valleys to dry plains, the Big Island's diversity offers a journey like no other.

Maximizing Your Island Hopping Experience

While Kauai provides a multitude of activities and experiences, island hopping enables you to widen your Hawaiian vacation even more. By planning day visits to other islands, you may design a variety of itineraries that suit your interests. Whether you're intrigued by the busy urban area of Oahu, the outdoor beauties of Maui, or the geological marvels of the Big Island, each island provides its own particular appeal and attraction.

A World of Possibilities Awaits

As you enjoy Kauai's natural beauty, rich culture, and local customs, consider extending your vacation by going to the surrounding islands. Island hopping from Kauai gives you a world of choices, enabling you to immerse yourself in the distinct character of each island and create a genuinely remarkable Hawaiian experience. Whether you want to soak in the sun on Waikiki Beach, watch a sunrise from the peak of a volcano, or venture into the heart of Polynesian culture, the wonder of Hawaii's islands awaits.

Soul-Refreshing Escapade

- Beyond its breathtaking beauty and exhilarating adventures, Kauai offers a soul-refreshing escapade from the hustle and bustle of everyday life. The tranquil ambiance, surrounded by nature's wonders, allows you to unwind and rejuvenate your spirit, leaving you with cherished memories to carry home.

Kauai is a true tropical haven that embraces travelers with its unique charm and enchanting beauty. Whether you seek outdoor adventures, cultural immersion, or peaceful relaxation, the Garden Isle offers a diverse array of experiences that cater to every traveler's desires. Embark on a journey to Kauai, and you'll find yourself immersed in the aloha spirit and the unparalleled splendor of this island paradise. Embrace the magic of Kauai, and it will undoubtedly hold a special place in your heart forever. Aloha and farewell!

Chapter Fifteen

Recommended Itineraries for Solo, Family and Friends

Kauai, the Garden Isle, offers a diverse range of activities and attractions to suit travelers of all ages and interests. In this chapter, we present recommended itineraries for different types of travelers, ensuring that everyone can make the most of their time on this breathtaking island. Whether you are a solo adventurer, a family with kids, or seeking family-friendly activities, Kauai has something special in store for you.

1. Solo Traveler Activities and Attractions

As a solo traveler, Kauai provides the perfect opportunity for self-discovery, adventure, and relaxation. Here are some must-visit attractions and activities tailored to the solo experience:

- Nā Pali Coast State Wilderness Park: Embark on a thrilling solo hike along the Kalalau Trail, offering jaw-dropping vistas of dramatic cliffs, lush valleys, and pristine beaches.

- Waimea Canyon: Known as the "Grand Canyon of the Pacific," solo travelers can explore Waimea Canyon's numerous trails, like the Cliff Trail, to witness the kaleidoscope of colors and awe-inspiring scenery.

- Hanalei Bay: Solo travelers looking to unwind can spend a day at Hanalei Bay, lounging on the beach, trying out water sports, and enjoying the laid-back vibe of the charming town.

- Helicopter Tour: Take to the skies on a thrilling helicopter tour of the island, capturing breathtaking aerial views of Kauai's iconic landscapes, including waterfalls, valleys, and hidden gems.

- Hanapepe Art Night: On Fridays, solo travelers can immerse themselves in local art and culture at Hanapepe Art Night, featuring galleries, live music, and delicious street food.

Traveling with Family and Kids Activities and Attractions

Kauai is a family-friendly destination, brimming with activities that will engage and entertain travelers of all ages. Here are some memorable experiences for families with kids:

- Wailua River Cruise: Hop on a scenic boat tour along the Wailua River to Fern Grotto, a natural lava rock cave with fern-covered walls. The kids will love the boat ride and the enchanting surroundings.

- Poipu Beach Park: Spend quality family time at Poipu Beach Park, where little ones can play in the gentle waves and parents can relax on the golden sands.

- Kauai Plantation Railway: Enjoy a leisurely train ride through the lush Kilohana Plantation, complete with farm animals and tropical gardens, providing a delightful experience for children.

- Kauai Children's Discovery Museums: Let the kids unleash their curiosity at the Kauai Children's Discovery Museum, featuring interactive exhibits and educational play areas.

- Limahuli Garden & Preserve: Take a guided tour of Limahuli Garden & Preserve, where the whole family can learn about native Hawaiian plants, cultural practices, and conservation efforts.

Family-Friendly Activities and Attractions

For families seeking activities that cater to both adults and children, Kauai boasts numerous attractions perfect for bonding experiences. Consider these family-friendly options:

- Kilauea Point National Wildlife Refuge: Visit the refuge and witness the majestic Lighthouse, spot migratory birds, and learn about the island's diverse wildlife.

- Spouting Horn: Marvel at the natural wonder of Spouting Horn, where waves crash into lava tubes, creating impressive water sprays and unique sounds.

- Kauai Coffee Company: Families can tour the Kauai Coffee Company plantation, sample delicious coffee, and stroll through the picturesque coffee fields.

- Luau Experience: Treat the whole family to an authentic Hawaiian luau, complete with traditional dances, music, and a delicious feast.

- Koke'e State Park: Explore Koke'e State Park together, featuring stunning lookouts, hiking trails, and opportunities for a family picnic amidst nature's beauty.

Childcare Facilities and Services

While Kauai is a family-friendly destination, parents may occasionally wish for some adult-only time to explore other attractions or enjoy a romantic dinner. Thankfully, the island offers reliable childcare facilities and services:

- Resort Kids' Clubs: Many resorts on Kauai have Kids' Clubs with supervised activities, games, and crafts, providing a safe and fun environment for children.

- Licensed Babysitters: Several licensed babysitting services are available on the island, ensuring professional care for your little ones.

- Resort In-room Childcare: Some resorts offer in-room childcare services, allowing parents to have a worry-free evening while their kids are looked after in the comfort of their room.

- Recommendations from Locals: Reach out to local families or resort staff for trusted recommendations on reliable and experienced childcare providers.

Kauai's diversity ensures that every traveler, whether solo or with family, will find captivating experiences and activities to suit their preferences.

From thrilling adventures along the Nā Pali Coast to serene moments at Poipu Beach Park, and from educational journeys at the Kauai Children's Discovery Museum to romantic luaus under the stars, Kauai caters to every desire.

Parents can also rest easy knowing that childcare services are available for times when adults wish to explore the island on their own. Embrace the enchantment of Kauai and cherish the memories created with loved ones amidst the island's breathtaking beauty and cultural richness.

Chapter Sixteen

Travel Tips and Etiquette

When visiting Kauai, it is necessary to be aware of the dos and don'ts to guarantee a polite and pleasurable experience for both guests and natives. Kauai boasts a strong cultural legacy and a vulnerable ecology, making it vital for travelers to adopt responsible travel practices. This chapter will go into in-depth information and comprehension of the dos and don'ts when vacationing on Kauai, along with the necessity of respectful conduct towards the island's population and environment.

Dos While Traveling in Kauai

1. Respect Local Traditions and Culture: Embrace the Hawaiian culture and traditions by studying about them before your vacation. Show reverence for holy locations, objects, and rituals that bear cultural importance to the island's population.

2. Support Local Businesses: Patronize local businesses, restaurants, and artists to help the island's economy and retain its distinctive community spirit.

3. Practice Sustainable Tourism: Reduce your environmental impact by selecting eco-friendly excursions and lodgings.

Avoid single-use plastics and help preserve Kauai's unspoiled natural beauty.

4. Learn and Use Basic Hawaiian Phrases: Show respect for the local language and culture by learning basic greetings and phrases. Locals will appreciate your attempts to connect with their history.

5. Adhere to the Leave No Trace Principles: When experiencing Kauai's natural beauties, always leave the environment as you found it. Avoid trash, remain on defined routes, and stop harassing animals.

6. Be Punctual and Respectful of Time: Hawaiians emphasize punctuality, so be on time for planned events and trips. Avoid excessive noise during quiet hours to promote a tranquil atmosphere for everyone.

7. Extend the Aloha Spirit: Embrace the Hawaiian notion of "Aloha" by sharing kindness and respect. Greet locals with a welcoming smile and treat them as you would want to be treated.

8. Ask for Permission for Photography: When shooting images of locals or at cultural events, ask for their approval first. Respect their privacy and cultural norms connected to photography.

9. Observe Traffic and Road Etiquette: Drive carefully and adhere to traffic restrictions. Yield to pedestrians and be mindful of other vehicles to provide a safe and enjoyable driving experience.

10. Participate in Cultural Activities: Engage in cultural events, seminars, and performances to acquire insight into Kauai's rich legacy and customs

11. Practice Ocean Safety: If you want to swim or participate in water activities, observe ocean safety standards. Heed warnings from lifeguards, stay careful of currents, and never turn your back on the water.

Don'ts While Traveling in Kauai

1. Don't Remove or Disturb Natural Resources: It is prohibited to remove rocks, shells, or other natural resources from beaches and parks. Leave them unspoiled for others to enjoy, and help protect the ecology.

2. Don't Trespass on Private Property: Respect borders and avoid trespassing on private grounds. Stick to specified public spaces and get permission when required.

3. Avoid Wearing Inappropriate Attire: When visiting holy places or attending cultural activities, avoid wearing revealing or insulting clothes. Dress modestly to demonstrate regard for the location or event.

4. Don't Touch or Harass Wildlife: Kauai is home to rare and sensitive species. Refrain from handling or feeding animals, since it might interrupt their normal behavior and risk their well-being.

5. Refrain from Loud or Disruptive activity: Maintain a serene and tranquil atmosphere by avoiding loud music, screaming, or disruptive activity, particularly in quiet and residential settings.

6. Don't Use Drones Without Permission: Flying drones in particular places may be forbidden owing to privacy and safety concerns. Obtain the required licenses before operating a drone on the island.

7. Avoid Taking Lava rocks: Hawaiian tradition indicates that taking lava rocks brings ill luck. Avoid collecting any volcanic rocks as mementos to respect local beliefs.

8: Don't Feed animals: Feeding animals may severely affect their natural foraging activities and lead to reliance on human food, which can be hazardous to their health.

9. Refrain from Standing on Coral Reefs: Coral reefs are fragile ecosystems that sustain a variety of marine life.

Stepping or standing on coral may cause irreversible harm. Swim and snorkel with caution.

10. Don't Drive Off-Road: Stick to approved roads and avoid off-roading since it might harm sensitive ecosystems and contribute to erosion.

Respectful Behavior toward Locals and Nature

Kauai's population, known as Kama'aina, greatly appreciates their history, traditions, and relationship to the land. As a guest, demonstrating respect for inhabitants and nature is vital to developing strong connections and conserving the island's culture and ecosystem.

1. Understanding the Aloha Spirit: The Aloha Spirit is a vital part of Hawaiian culture, stressing compassion, love, and harmony with people and the environment. Embrace this energy in your encounters with locals and while visiting the island.

Page|191

2. Greeting with Aloha: Use "Aloha" as a greeting, which implies welcome, farewell, and love. Extend this kind of welcome to residents and other guests equally to build a welcoming environment.

3. Seeking Permission for Sacred Sites: Some spots on Kauai, such as Heiau (ancient Hawaiian temples) and culturally important sites, possess spiritual value. Always ask for permission before visiting or taking pictures at these sites.

4. Attending Cultural Events with Respect: If you attend cultural events, plays, or festivals, show respect by listening carefully, obeying directions, and abstaining from disruptive conduct.

5. Contributing to Local Customs: Participate in cultural activities with humility and respect. For example, if you're invited to a traditional ceremony, learn about the acceptable etiquette beforehand.

6. Preserving Natural Spaces: Kauai's magnificent landscapes and marine life are vulnerable ecosystems. Ensure their preservation by obeying all park laws, remaining on specified trails, and not destroying any natural resources.

7. Supporting Local Artisans: Appreciate and support local artists and craftsmen by buying their handcrafted items or visiting art festivals and exhibits.

8. Showing Gratitude: Express thanks to locals who share their culture, expertise, and hospitality with you. A simple "mahalo" (thank you) may go a long way.

By sticking to these dos and don'ts and adopting polite conduct, you will not only have a more enjoyable trip experience but also contribute to the preservation of Kauai's natural beauty and unique culture for future generations to enjoy.

Chapter Seventeen

Language Guide

Common Phrases and Expressions

The Garden Isle is a wonderful place that provides not only amazing natural beauty but also a rich cultural experience. While English is commonly spoken on the island, knowing a few local words and expressions will considerably improve your trip experience and help you connect with the kind and inviting islanders. In this chapter, we will give you 30 helpful terms and phrases in the local language, giving you a look into the heart of Kauai's culture and helping you to immerse yourself in the island's distinctive ambiance.

1. Aloha: Arguably the most renowned Hawaiian term, "aloha" is used for both "hello" and "goodbye." It also reflects the spirit of love, care, and compassion.

2. Mahalo: This term means "thank you." Use it to show your thanks to the people for their hospitality and friendliness.

3. Ohana: "Ohana" translates to "family" and goes beyond blood relatives, embracing close friends and anybody considered part of your inner circle.

4. Pau Hana: Literally meaning "finished work," "Pau hana" refers to the period after work when individuals rest and mingle.

5. Honu is The Hawaiian term for "turtle," and green sea turtles may frequently be sighted swimming around Kauai's coasts.

6. Pupu: These are appetizers or nibbles commonly taken before a meal or during happy hour.

7. Hale: "Hale" means "house" or "home," and you'll commonly encounter it in the names of lodgings and resorts.

8. Mahina: "Mahina" means "moon" in Hawaiian. Keep an eye out for unique moonlight activities and festivities around the island.

9. Malihini: Referring to immigrants or guests, "malihini" is a phrase that differentiates people who are not native to the islands.

10. Kama'aina: On the other hand, "kama'aina" refers to long-term inhabitants or locals.

11. 'Ono: This term simply means "delicious" and is commonly used to describe the island's wonderful food.

12. Mano: "Mano" translates to "shark," and although you may not want to meet one in the seas, understanding the phrase can be beneficial for safety considerations.

13. Mauka and Makai: "Mauka" means "toward the mountains," while "makai" means "toward the ocean." These directional phrases are regularly used on the island.

14. Lanai: "Lanai" is a patio or balcony, a fantastic location to relax and enjoy the gorgeous views.

15. Pono: "Pono" denotes justice, balance, and harmony, a basic value in Hawaiian culture.

16. Kapu: Meaning "forbidden" or "off-limits," "kapu" signs are erected in select regions to preserve holy sites.

17. Lei: A garland of flowers or leaves that is typically provided as a loving welcome or farewell gift.

18. Hula: The ancient Hawaiian dance that recounts tales via beautiful movements and gestures

19. 'Iwa: Known as the big frigatebird, the "iwa" is a spectacular bird commonly seen flying over Kauai's coasts.

20. Makani: "Makani" refers to "wind," and the island's trade winds produce delightful breezes.

21. Nalu: "Nalu" means "wave" and is great for surfers seeking to catch some of Kauai's legendary waves.

22. Mele: "Mele" refers to music or singing and is a vital aspect of Hawaiian culture and events.

23. Pali: A steep cliff or slope, and you'll find stunning pali vistas when touring the island.

24. Pua: "Pua" indicates "flower," and the island's lush vegetation includes numerous vivid and fragrant blooms.

25. Wahine and Kane: "Wahine" means "woman," while "kane" means "man." These terms are typically used to allude to genders.

26. Haleakala: Though Kauai is not home to this famed volcano, "Haleakala" means "House of the Sun" and is situated on Maui.

27. Kaukau: "Kaukau" simply means "food," and you'll be thrilled by the numerous gastronomic possibilities on the island.

28. Heiau: Ancient Hawaiian temples or holy locations where rites were done

29. Kokua: "Kokua" refers to "help" or "assistance," representing the sense of community and collaboration in Hawaii.

30. Hana Hou: Literally "encore" or "one more time," "hana hou" is used to request an extra performance or a repetition of anything nice.

Learning these fundamental Hawaiian terms and phrases can not only enrich your trip experience but also show the locals that you cherish their culture and traditions. The people of Kauai are proud of their language and customs, and your attempts to embrace their way of life will be warmly acknowledged.

What Makes Kauai a Unique Destination

Kauai stands out among Hawaii's islands for various reasons, making it a genuinely unique and fascinating destination.

Unspoiled Natural Beauty: As the oldest and northernmost of the major Hawaiian Islands, Kauai's lush landscapes have remained largely unspoiled, retaining a feeling of pure beauty and solitude.

The Na Pali Coast: Kauai's famed Na Pali Coast is a geological wonder with its steep cliffs, deep valleys, and emerald green flora. The mountainous coastline is only accessible by foot, boat, or air, making it a marvel to see.

"Jurassic" Landscape: Kauai's magnificent beauty has made it a preferred site for countless blockbuster films, including the legendary "Jurassic Park" trilogy. The island's primordial appeal and surreal beauty have caught the minds of filmmakers and vacationers alike.

Spiritual Energy: Kauai is commonly referred to as the "healing island," owing to the feeling of spiritual energy and tranquility that pervades its surroundings. Many think that the island's natural environs possess a unique and strong energy that stimulates rejuvenation and connection with nature.

Traditional Hawaiian Lifestyle: Kauai is one of the few areas in Hawaii where the traditional Hawaiian lifestyle and cultural traditions continue to flourish. The island's population has deep links to their ancestry, and tourists may experience true Hawaiian traditions and beliefs.

The Wettest Place on Earth: Mount Waialeale, situated in the middle of Kauai, is one of the wettest areas in the world.

The mountain's plentiful rainfall adds to the island's beautiful flora and many waterfalls.

Spiritual and holy Sites: Kauai is home to several holy sites, including ancient temples known as heiau, that give an insight into the island's rich cultural past and religious rituals.

Secluded and Private Getaways: Kauai provides a choice of secluded and private lodgings, including lovely cottages, luxurious villas, and romantic beachfront resorts, giving an intimate getaway from the outside world.

Napali Coast Wilderness Park: This UNESCO World Heritage Site comprises the rocky coastline and interior of the Na Pali Coast, offering protection to the various ecosystems and cultural legacy of the region.

Warm and Welcoming Locals: The people of Kauai are noted for their genuine warmth and friendliness, making tourists feel like they are part of the extended ohana (family) from the time they arrive.

Preservation of Nature: The island's dedication to maintaining its natural beauty and reducing environmental effects is apparent in its attempts to preserve the delicate balance between tourism and conservation.

Rich Cultural Traditions: The island's cultural traditions, including hula, music, and storytelling, are actively handed down through generations, enabling visitors to experience the spirit of Hawaiian culture.

Different Microclimates: Kauai's different microclimates contribute to a diversity of landscapes, from lush rainforests to desert canyons, allowing a range of outdoor activities for guests to enjoy.

Adventure and Exploration: Whether you're trekking along gorgeous trails, kayaking through secret streams, or snorkeling in vivid reefs, Kauai provides a multitude of adventure activities for thrill-seekers and nature aficionados.

Mana: The Hawaiian idea of "mana" refers to spiritual energy and strength. Many visitors to Kauai feel a sense of amazement and wonder, frequently attributing it to the island's powerful mana.

Personal Testimonials and Stories from Tourists

Countless tourists have fallen in love with Kauai's beautiful scenery, welcoming culture, and remarkable experiences. Let me share some of the personal testimonies and anecdotes I received via email from people who have been enchanted by the Garden Isle's allure:

"Hey, Great Man! James
My visit to Kauai was a life-changing experience. The moment I set foot on the island, I felt an overwhelming sense of tranquility and peace. Exploring the Na Pali Coast by boat was like stepping into a dream, with towering cliffs, hidden sea caves, and playful dolphins surrounding us. The locals' hospitality was heartwarming, and I'll always cherish the memories of dancing hula with new friends during a traditional luau. Kauai's natural beauty touched my soul, and I left the island feeling rejuvenated and connected to nature in a profound way."
Sarah, USA

"Kauai exceeded all my expectations as a wildlife enthusiast. The island's diverse ecosystems provided me with opportunities to spot rare birds, including the elusive 'iwa soaring above the ocean. Hiking through Waimea Canyon was like entering another world, with its vibrant reds and greens contrasting against the clear blue sky. The immense mana I felt during my time on Kauai was unlike anything I've ever experienced, and it left me in awe of the island's spiritual energy." David, UK

"Hello, Mr. James
I'll never forget my solo trip to Kauai, where I found myself immersed in the true meaning of aloha. The locals' genuine kindness and welcoming spirit made me feel like a part of their extended family. One evening, I attended a traditional storytelling session at a heiau, and the ancient tales woven with dance and music were both moving and enlightening. Watching the sunrise from the top of Sleeping Giant Trail brought tears to my eyes as I witnessed nature's breathtaking beauty unfolding before me." Maria, Spain

"Good morning, Mr. James Vollmer.
Thank you for your email. Messages I received from you during my last visit to Kauai indicated that Kauai provided the perfect

setting for a romantic getaway with my partner. We explored hidden waterfalls hand in hand and shared laughter while paddleboarding along the serene Hanalei River. The island's secluded beaches allowed us to enjoy intimate picnics and watch the sunset in peaceful solitude. We fell in love not only with Kauai's stunning landscapes but also with each other all over again." Michael and Emily, Australia

"Hi

My Experience in Kauai was awesome. As a food enthusiast, Kauai was a culinary paradise for me. The farmers' markets showcased an abundance of fresh tropical fruits and unique treats, while the seafood offerings at local restaurants were simply divine. I even had the opportunity to join a cooking class and learn traditional Hawaiian recipes, infusing my meals with the flavors and spirit of the island. Thank you, sir.

"Aisha, UAE

Chapter Eighteen

Extra-Useful Facts

Local Festivals and Celebrations

Kauai's cultural diversity is celebrated throughout the year with numerous festivals and events that provide tourists with a look into the island's traditions and customs. Some of the prominent festivals and events on Kauai include:

Waimea Town Celebration: Held in February, this week-long celebration remembers the island's heritage and incorporates rodeo competitions, live music, hula performances, and a colorful procession.

Prince Kuhio Day: Celebrated in March, this festival celebrates Prince Jonah Kuhio Kalaniana'ole, a renowned figure in Hawaiian history and a driving force behind the island's preservation efforts.

Kauai Polynesian Festival: This yearly festival in May celebrates the Polynesian cultures via dance, music, arts, and crafts, creating a compelling cultural experience.

Eo E Emalani I Alakai event: Taking place in October, this event celebrates Queen Emma with a trek to Kokee State Park, where a recreation of her trip is staged.

The Unique Flora and Fauna of Kauai

Kauai's seclusion and different microclimates have given birth to a large assortment of unique flora and animals that can be found nowhere else in the world. Some of the island's notable plant and animal species include:

Kauai Amakihi: This little, colorful bird is native to the island and is regularly sighted in Kauai's jungles.

Kokee Mints: These unusual plants, also known as Clermontia peleana, have stunning red blossoms and are located in the upper altitudes of Kokee State Park.

Silversword: This stunning silver-hued plant, Argyroxiphium sandwicense, may be spotted in the alpine parts of Kauai, flourishing in the volcanic soil.

Nene: The nene, or Hawaiian goose, is the state bird of Hawaii and may be observed on Kauai, notably at Kilauea Point National Wildlife Refuge.

Moa: The endangered Hawaiian gallinule, commonly known as moa, may be found in wetland regions on the island.

Kauai's Contributions to the Film Industry

Kauai's stunning vistas have long been sought after by filmmakers, and the island has played a vital role in the film industry. Some of the noteworthy films filmed on Kauai include:

Jurassic Park: The lush forests and towering waterfalls of Kauai served as the scene for the renowned "Jurassic Park" movie trilogy.

South Pacific: The picturesque Hanalei Bay gave the ideal location for the great musical "South Pacific."

Pirates of the Caribbean: The spectacular cliffs of the Na Pali Coast were included in multiple "Pirates of the Caribbean" films, providing an exciting dimension to the flicks.

Indiana Jones: Kauai's stunning scenery was also employed in the "Indiana Jones" series, contributing to the spirit of exploration and adventure.

Island Hopping and Day Trips from Kauai

While Kauai has a wealth of sights and activities, island hopping and day excursions enable tourists to discover nearby islands and enhance their Hawaiian experience.

Some popular day excursions and adjacent islands to consider are:

Niihau: Known as the "Forbidden Island," Niihau is privately owned and inaccessible to most travelers. However, helicopter flights give overhead views of this remote and culturally valuable island.

Oahu: Take a short trip to Oahu to enjoy the busy city life of Honolulu, tour Pearl Harbor, and explore renowned attractions such as Waikiki Beach and Diamond Head.
Maui: Fly to Maui to experience the dawn from the peak of Haleakala, tour the verdant Hana Road, and dive in the crystal-clear waters of Molokini Crater.

Big Island: Discover the various landscapes of Hawaii's Big Island, including the active volcanoes of Hawaii Volcanoes National Park and the beautiful valleys of Waipio and Pololu.
Land hopping and day visits give a unique chance to see the

variety of Hawaii's islands, each boasting its own particular beauty and cultural richness.

With this complete book, you are now well-equipped to go on an incredible vacation to Kauai, the Garden Isle. From learning local words and embracing the aloha spirit to immersing yourself in the island's distinctive flora and wildlife, Kauai offers a memorable trip that will leave you with treasured memories for a lifetime.

As you explore the stunning scenery, interact with the warm-hearted residents, and experience the island's lively culture, may you find yourself linked to the genuine soul of Hawaii. Whether you want leisure on quiet beaches, adventurous activities in the great outdoors, or a better knowledge of Hawaiian customs, Kauai has something to offer every tourist.

Conclusion

Kauai, the Garden Isle of Hawaii, is a wonderfully unique and lovely place that makes a lasting impact on everyone who comes. With its unspoiled natural beauty, rich cultural legacy, kind friendliness, and wealth of outdoor experiences, Kauai delivers an experience unlike any other. From exploring the craggy Na Pali Coast to immersing oneself in the island's spiritual essence, every minute on Kauai is a voyage of discovery and connection with nature and the local people.

As you plan your vacation to Kauai, embrace the spirit of aloha and immerse yourself in the island's ancient rituals and way of life. Learning a few local words can improve your relationship with the warm-hearted folks and demonstrate your admiration for their culture.

From the spectacular cliffs of the Na Pali Coast to the lush jungles and hidden beaches, Kauai's scenery will steal your breath away at every turn. As the sun sets over the Pacific Ocean, painting the sky with bright colors, you'll experience a feeling of peace and awe that will linger with you long after you say aloha to the Garden Isle.

Embark on a trip to Kauai, where ancient traditions meet modern-day marvels and where the spirit of aloha welcomes you to enjoy the genuine essence of Hawaii. Discover the charm of Kauai, the Garden Isle, and create memories that will live in your heart forever. Mahalo for joining us on this incredible excursion, and may your travels be blessed with pleasure, adventure, and aloha.

As you say goodbye to the Garden Isle, may the spirit of aloha linger in your heart, leading you on future adventures and developing a lasting love for Kauai and its magnificent beauty.

Safe travels, and until we meet again, a hui hou! Aloha!

Made in the USA
Monee, IL
27 May 2025

18258853R00125